GENERAL AND COMMUNICATIONS STUDIES

Don't You Believe It!

Macmillan Technician Series

Peter Astley, *Engineering, Drawing and Design II*

P. J. Avard and J. Cross, *Workshop Processes and Materials I*

G. D. Bishop, *Electrical and Electronic Systems and Practice I*

G. D. Bishop, *Electronics II*

G. D. Bishop, *Electronics III*

Don Carroll, *General and Communications Studies*

J. C. Cluley, *Electrical Drawing I*

John Elliott, *Building Science and Materials*

John G. Ellis and Norman J. Riches, *Safety and Laboratory Practice*

D. E. Hewitt, *Engineering Science II*

P. R. Lancaster and D. Mitchell, *Mechanical Science III*

Rhys Lewis, *Physical Science I*

Noel M. Morris, *Digital Techniques*

Noel M. Morris, *Electrical Principles II*

Noel M. Morris, *Electrical Principles III*

Owen Perry and Joyce Perry, *Mathematics I*

A. Simpson, *Light Current Electrical Applications III*

GENERAL AND COMMUNICATIONS STUDIES

Don't You Believe It!

Don Carroll

M

© Don Carroll 1981

All rights reserved. No part of this publication may be reproduced or transmitted, in any form or by any means, without permission

First published 1981 by
THE MACMILLAN PRESS LTD
London and Basingstoke
Associated companies in Delhi Dublin
Hong Kong Johannesburg Lagos Melbourne
New York Singapore and Tokyo

ISBN 0 333 29462 9

Printed in Hong Kong

The paperback edition of this book is sold subject to the condition that it shall not, by way of trade or otherwise, be lent, resold, hired out, or otherwise circulated without the publisher's prior consent in any form of binding or cover other than that in which it is published and without a similar condition including this condition being imposed on the subsequent purchaser.

Contents

Preface vi

Introduction vii

LEVEL 1

Subject Area: The System 2

Topic 1	Rights and procedure during arrest	4
Topic 2	A case of murder: You, the jury	6
Topic 3	We've got you taped	9
Topic 4	The Welfare State/Social Myth – What is falsely obvious	18
Topic 5	Forms of language within the system	27

Subject Area: Social Relations 31

Topic 1	'Am I an Image?'	31
Topic 2a	Women's work and apprenticeships	34
Topic 2b	Equal pay and the law	41
Topic 3	Mixing it!	47
Topic 4	Something larger than me	55
Topic 5	Power relations between the sexes	59

LEVEL 2

Subject Area: Mass Communications 68

Topic 1	The Press	70
Topic 2	Turn your radio on	72
Topic 3	The *Star* – Porn or Pawn?	76
Topic 4	Television – Viewers' Droop?	81

Subject Area: Political Literacy 83

Topic 1	Politics, what politics?	83
Topic 2	Wealth/Poverty: Income/Outcome	86
Topic 3	Who owns Britain? Distribution of wealth and income	89
Topic 4	Paying through the tax system	93
Topic 5	Taxation–Avoidance and evasion	95

LEVEL 3

Subject Area: Ideology 100

Topic 1	Standpoints of History	100
Topic 2	Caught in a catch-phrase (including history/herstory)	101
Topic 3	Making your Mark	103
Topic 4	Making up your mind… (for you)	104
Topic 5	The old school tie	107
Topic 6	Freedom of the editorial	109
Topic 7	Equality – More equal than whom?	111

Preface

The material is divided as follows:
Levels 1, 2 and 3 are divided into *Subject Areas*.
These Subject Areas are then subdivided into various *Topics*.

The aims at the start of each Subject Area apply throughout each Topic within the Subject Area as well as the aims prefacing some individual Topics.

Though the material is designed to cohere, focus and interconnect, it will be possible to use topics in part or out of sequence.

The occasional note/advice that applies specifically to lecturers is indicated by ● in the margin.

The book, as a whole, is aimed at students doing TEC courses. Though it is hoped that the material is systematic *and* demanding, it clearly cannot claim to peddle any panaceas. There may, as always, be some odd reactions from students. Lecturers should remember that a student attitude is not necessarily a conviction: build enticing bricks of contradiction.

Dedicated to the best TEC General and Communications Studies aim I've seen:
'That students see themselves as part of a historical process: as products and producers'.

Acknowledgement

In no society is any product the exclusive result of one person's effort.

John Berger

Introduction

An essential feature of the Department of Education and Science Circular 323, in 1957, was the suggestion that education provided in Further Education was generally too limited in concept. Linking subject areas, which modified traditional subject boundaries and developed a trend away from excessive specialisation were required. These subject areas would need to be more contrasting and would need to recognise the fuller, personal development of the student. To provide for this, General Studies would need to embody a mixture of subjects and would require an interdisciplinary approach.

The material in this book has been drawn from as wide a range of topics and interests as possible. It has been selected because it relates directly to the student following a TEC course and has direct inroads into his or her experience.

As regards the teacher, a commensurate interest in those diverse aspects of human behaviour that are being demanded of the student, is essential. For practical purposes, this type of interdisciplinary energy is best embodied in the form of imaginative scissors: the real work of preparation and teaching is to cohere and focus this diverse material.

The Consumer

As a starting point, General Studies lecturers should recognise some of the contradictory characteristics of those students who will receive General Studies. They are a result of the contradictions of the society from which they come.

They include an unquestioning disposal towards a compete and rise culture; the (commonly passed on) identification of their own subject area as constituting the totality of education; deliberately created ignorance as a form of social control, politics, for example, having been turned into a disenfranchising blizzard of trivia. Personality clashes in Parliament have appropriated the word 'politics' with the result that nothing else is seen to be 'political'.

There is no systematic exposing to counter information or critical questioning of available forms of information which creates and reinforces prevailing social and political attitudes.

Simultaneously, those who receive General Studies also exhibit a strong, if not singing sense of the self and a sustained reaction against the denial of overall knowledge that much work can represent.

Though Training is clearly necessary, it should not be confused with Education. Life is more than livelihood. In this sense, General Studies is not a confirming subject. It is much more combative. It is an attempt to create a critical awareness, initially through the presentation of information that exposes the student to contradictions, socially, culturally and politically; information that would be difficult to observe, digest, analyse and discuss elsewhere.

For many students in Further Education, General Studies is their second and maybe final attempt at social sense-making: the ultimate enfranchisement is critical control over their own lives. This is the level of the task.

Methodology

A cruel word for 'how'

There has been much agonising over whether 'Communication Skills' is part of General Studies or whether 'Communication Skills' actually makes General Studies redundant. This has been compounded in the Technician Education Council General Studies submissions by the fact that they are General *and* Communication Studies submissions. Prior to the establishment of TEC, the extremes of each independent position were, for Communication Skills, a behavioural paradise of workplace programming at the expense of General Studies; and for General Studies, a rhapsodic, deliberately unplanned, let-it-all-hang-out-and-what-is-print-anyway approach.

The approach here makes the following assumptions:
technically, General Studies appropriates Communications. A student cannot communicate without communicating *something*. *What* is being communicated is as important as *how*. The form of communication should be encouraged and developed through content. Clearly, General Studies should have as part of its aims, the improving of general communicating competence but the form and content are not divisible. Thus, this material will test the educational aims and objectives *through* the content.

There is little point in stating a General and Communication Studies programme without specifying a teaching method, or cutting edge for actual teaching purposes. The method here involves an attempt to marry common aims and objectives, culled from many TEC submissions, to material which has been lying around available to General Studies before but which has not, as yet, been given a general teaching framework. One teaching method which has been successful has been to use material which embodies comparison and contrast. This elucidates and illustrates contradictions. Information received through the usual sources by students is rarely objective fact; it is commonly presented from some standpoint which is not explicitly stated. Frequently this information serves an ideological function. One example is the obsession of certain papers with 'scroungers' while hardly any publicity is given to the amount of unclaimed welfare benefit or the amount of tax evasion.

The effect of this is that students are not nurtured on balance, nor are their reasoning capacities courted let alone adequately developed. Though much of the information they receive is manifestly partial, they are, none the less, asked to come to judgement on many issues. General Studies has a role here in promoting balance: thus, the importance of content.

The material in this book should not be merely a process of handing on information that is commonly available elsewhere. If so, there would be hardly any point in compiling it. Any information conveyed to students *must* be complemented with a rigorous approach which promotes a critical awareness of the overall society of which the student is a part. The material begins with information-based questions but soon becomes more open-ended. Ultimately, a form of literacy should be developed embracing reading and writing abilities to achieve a *political* literacy.

Starting the Term

Alternatively, what exactly are you looking for?

Commence exactly as you mean to continue.
This means alerting the students to what *you* will be doing and *how* it will be done before soliciting from them what they might want to do.
The overall objective here is to promote a critical awareness; this can only be fruitfully done by promoting a critical method.
There is little point in being approximate and sloppy in teaching preparation if one is demanding that the student avoid being precisely that.

Though every teacher has his or her treasured handouts, it can be difficult at the start of the year to find something to deliver to the students which is engaging *and* heuristic, concrete *and* prompting. For a group who have never met before, perhaps never been involved in a general discussion, and whose ages might vary, it is important to locate material which not only generates interest but which will encourage contributions, however tentative. The topic selected, or the content of the material, at this stage, should not be too remote from the collective experience of the students. This should facilitate the initial aim of developing an atmosphere which can provide a fruitful sense of being listened to, for all the students.

When one observes the complicated and almost mathematical assessments of personality on some TEC specification sheets, it can be too easily forgotten that a willingness to receive and a recognition of the effect on others should be seen as the essential lubricants for communication: a necessary oxygen, without which there might well be none.

For groups who range from being slightly inhibited, or even prone to a strangling silence or even those who have found their central core, it is recommended that the year commence with a topic area that is relatively objective. (General Studies is, above all, the one area where the 'relatively objective' can, with a little fine-tuning, be readily seen as the incestuous cousin of the notoriously subjective.)

The starting material recommended here has a successful pedigree. It is a useful 'hook' because it relates the law as it could, and, in many cases has, affected the student. There is nothing distancing or exceptional about this. There may be individual knowledge but little in detail, or collectively, about the law. On the other hand, nothing loosens the tongue more than *incidents* about the law. They are the skeleton to which almost any flesh may be added.

Charisma

Or, the life and soul of the Arty.

Everything has its use. Charisma may well be the ace that launched a thousand students through many Humanities departments but it has its limits. Successful General Studies teaching, that is the developing of the students' critical faculties, demands that the charismatic personality uses that talent to serve a purpose wider than itself.

Eventually the students will leave. It is better that they have grasped, through teaching, the transferable tools of critical judgement and method than have passively enjoyed observing somebody doing their thinking for them – and possibly, ultimately preventing them.

Again, the purpose of the material is to transfer a critical method so that eventually, the students can identify sharks from soap. Without this method, the charismatic personality becomes a container without freight; the teaching, a benevolent form of control.

Side effects

A plug for the Full Self

Much of this material is contrasting and 'vocational' in a sense wider than can be mechanically measured by 'skill' assessment or an answer to a series of multiple choice questions. Those in Further Education who use the term 'vocational' as the Ultimate Good and sole justification for any activity, however dubious, use it in a very restricted sense. It is as if students have been caught in the swing doors of some half open university and injected with 'usefulness', for which General Studies lecturers must continually find antidotes. The door *is*, in these circumstances only half open but that half is made to appear as the whole.

It is as well to be aware that the word 'vocational' as used functionally has no monopoly on what may or may not be useful to the student. The deliberate shredding of the student's total experience into 'vocational' and 'non-vocational' is always an artificial exercise. The TEC guidelines 3/75, continuing the June 1974 policy statement seemed to comply with this in stating:

> Although the young student in employment may gain most of his or her experience outside the college, such studies (G & CS) can help him or her to interpret that experience.

Even though the balance of time-spread for G & CS is 85 per cent parent department and 15 per cent G & CS, that experience should be seen as a whole; and the proportion of GS time should not minimise its importance.

People are more than what they produce even if they are the last to know it. The word 'vocational' should be reclaimed and applied to the whole process of growth, which all learning should be.

ACKNOWLEDGEMENTS....

The author and publishers wish to thank the following, who have kindly given permission for the use of copyright material:

BBC Publications for an extract, and two pictures by Sue and Hugh Ribbans from *Trade Union Studies 2*;
The Editor, News of the World, for the 'Comment' from the issue dated March 5th, 1978;
Guardian Newspapers Ltd., for extracts from *The Guardian*;
Labour Research Development for extracts from their publications;
Mirror Group Newspapers Ltd. for news extracts from the *Daily Mirror* and *Sunday Mirror*;
National Council for Civil Liberties for extracts from their pamphlets;
New Science Publications for extracts from *New Society*;
Quartet Books Ltd. for extracts from *The Gender Trap: A Closer Look at Sex Roles, Book 2 'Sex and Marriage'* by Carol Adams and Rae Laurikietis, published in association with Virago Ltd. 1976;
Rape Counselling and Research Project for an extract from their leaflet 'Rape and Fighting Back';
The Statesman & Nation Publishing Company Ltd. for extracts from 'Tories and Tax Myth' (13 April 1979) and 'Politics and the News: Distortion' (6 April 1979) published in the *New Statesman*;
Times Newspapers Ltd. for the article 'What The State Knows About You' from *The Sunday Times*, June 2, 1978;
Trades Union Congress for an extract from *Rights at Work*;
Virago Ltd. for extracts from *Taking Liberties*.

...and our thanks also to everyone else who contributed towards this book. Every effort has been made to trace all the copyright holders, but if any have been inadvertently overlooked, we offer our apologies, and invite them to contact the publishers to make the necessary arrangements.

Level 1

Subject Area: The System

Embarking Material How well do you know the Law?

This material may be used in different ways

(1) The questions may be posed and written answers sought from libraries etc.
(2) Answers could be sought from various rights and law centres, legal pamphlets etc.
(3) Information could be orally conveyed in a straightforward manner or phased to prompt the desire for more information.
(4) Further discussion could be stimulated about *the nature of the law*: do we need laws; are they too liberal or too repressive etc.
(5) They could be used to promote further reading. (Or any mixture of these.)

● The general aim is *not* to treat the questions in the form of yes/no answers but to convey and solicit information through discussion.

Aims

(1) To develop a command of the essential elements of communication through oral means.
(2) To listen to each other.

Read over and discuss

● The material may last two or three sessions. If it is clearly going on too long (depending on the response) finish the remaining questions briefly.
● Now *jointly* select three or four issues (or areas of further interest); these will be covered more comprehensively.

How well do you know the law?

(1) Are you legally obliged to go to the police station before you are charged?
(2) Are you legally obliged to answer police questions (a) before, (b) after arrest?
(3) Are you legally obliged to give your fingerprints to the police?
(4) Does a magistrate have to be legally trained?
(5) In court, does the defendant sit with his or her legal representative?
(6) Must a defendant be legally represented in court?
(7) What is the minimum age that you can be held responsible for a criminal offence in England and Wales?
(8) Does the verdict of a jury have to be unanimous?
(9) Under what circumstances may a prisoner marry while in prison?
(10) May a policeman or woman search you in the street without a warrant?
(11) May the police search your house without a warrant?
(12) If a 15 year old enters a pub and orders a pint, is he/she breaking the law?
(13) Can a girl under 16 have a legal abortion?
(14) Are there circumstances in which a girl under 18 may get married without her parents' consent?
(15) At what age may someone leave home and live where they like in whatever conditions they choose?
(16) In rented accommodation, can the landlord evict you at any time without notice?
(17) Can a shopkeeper claim his goods are selling at a reduced price if this is not true?
(18) If you are sent goods which you have not ordered can you keep them without paying?
(19) At what age can you have a credit card?
(20) What is the minimum age for persons serving on a jury?
(21) Can an employer (a) refuse to let you serve on a jury (b) refuse to pay you?

Topic 1 Procedure and rights during arrest

Aims

(1) To examine the nature of the law as it applies to the individual.
(2) To develop writing abilities.
(3) To summarise and elicit appropriate information.
(4) To grasp the thought and pattern of a work at the required level of generality.

Arrest
NCCL fact sheet 1

This fact sheet explains what powers the police have to arrest you and what your rights are.

Usually when the police ask for your assistance, you will want to help them. But you should know your rights and know when you are not legally obliged to co-operate.

If you are stopped by the police
Neither the police nor anyone else has a general power to stop you, make you answer questions or take you to a police station without arresting you. There is nothing to stop the police asking you questions, but in most cases you have no legal duty to answer.

The police can stop and search you in the streets, if they have reasonable grounds to think that you possess prohibited drugs, firearms, stolen goods (in some parts of the country) or anything connected with terrorism. The fact sheet on Search gives more details.

Giving your name and address
In the following situations, the police have the right to ask your name and address and you can be prosecuted for not giving it. If you don't give it, or if they think you have given a false name, you can be arrested.

You are driving a motor vehicle (in this case, the police also have the right to ask your age). If you refuse to give your name, you can be arrested if you are suspected of driving carelessly or dangerously.

You are suspected of creating a disturbance at a public meeting.

You are suspected of possessing prohibited drugs.

You possess a firearm and fail to produce a firearms certificate.

You are suspected of having an offensive weapon in a public place.

You fail to produce a ticket or pay the fare on a train.

At your place of work
If the police ask to see you at your workplace, get in touch immediately with your union representative. You should refuse to be questioned in your employer's presence.

Shoplifting
In law, any citizen has the right to arrest someone whom he sees committing an arrestable offence (see the section below for examples of these offences). This power is used by store detectives when they want to hold someone suspected of shoplifting. If you believe you've been wrongfully arrested, or if excessive force was used, you should get advice about taking legal action.

Mentally ill people
The police can take to a place of safety a mentally disordered person found in a public place who appears to be in immediate need of care and control, even if she or he has not committed a criminal offence.

'Helping the police with their enquiries'
People are often questioned at a police station without actually being arrested. If a policeman asks you to go to the police station, ask if he is arresting you. If he says 'no', then you can choose whether to go or not. But if you refuse to go, you may find yourself arrested anyway — and you shouldn't try and resist arrest by force.

If you go voluntarily to the police station, get a solicitor or some other independent person to go with you. Although you have a right to contact a friend or lawyer once you get to the station, this is usually difficult.

Arrest without a warrant
There are many situations where a police officer can arrest you *without* having a warrant from the magistrates' court. These are:

When he has reasonable cause to suspect that you have committed, are committing or about to commit an arrestable offence — ie an offence carrying a maximum penalty of at least 5 years' imprisonment and some other offences. This includes theft, most offences against the person, blackmail, unlawful possession of drugs, taking and driving away a vehicle, and many others.

When it is necessary to prevent or stop a breach of the peace.

If he reasonably suspects that you are obstructing the highway.

If you are suspected of possessing an offensive weapon.

If you refuse to take or fail to pass a breathalyser.

If you are suspected of being involved in terrorism.

If you are found drunk and incapable in a public place.

You must be told the reason for your arrest, unless you are caught red-handed or the reason is obvious.

Arrest with a warrant
If the police officer has a warrant for your arrest, ask to see it. If the arrest is for a debt — eg not paying maintenance — you must be shown the warrant before the arrest. If the arrest is for a criminal offence, you should be shown it or have it read to you — whichever you prefer — as soon as possible after your arrest.

Make sure the warrant really refers to you.

See whether the warrant gives instructions for you to be released on bail. If it does, the police must release you and tell you when to come to court.

Questioning
You have the right to REMAIN SILENT when the police question you. It is usually better to refuse to say anything or sign any statement except after getting legal advice. For more information, see fact sheet on Questioning.

At the police station
The police SHOULD:

Caution you that anything you say may be put down in writing and used as evidence.

Tell you as soon as possible what offences you are charged with.

Allow you to contact by phone or telegram your family, a friend or a lawyer, at your own expense.

Contact your family if you ask them to, to tell them where you are.

Allow you to talk to your solicitor out of their hearing.

Make reasonable arrangements for your comfort and refreshment.

Package and seal any property taken from you. You should
- make sure the property is listed and properly described
- check the list is correct
- sign below the last item on the list to prevent additions
- ask for a receipt and keep it.

The police should NOT

Compel you to answer any questions.

Hold out any promises (eg bail) or make any threats in order to get a statement.

Compel you to sign any statement.

Suggest that you plead guilty.

Force you to have your fingerprints taken without a court order.

Force you to take part in an ID parade.

If you are under 17, interview you without a parent or some other independent person being present.

These are your rights, although they are often denied by the police. If you are refused contact with your family, or pressured into giving a statement, or assaulted, you should get legal advice about taking action or making a complaint against the police.

Fingerprinting
The police have no right to take your fingerprints without your consent. After you have been charged with an offence, they can apply to a magistrates' court for an order allowing them to take finger or palm prints, even if you still refuse. They can use 'reasonable force' to take prints.

If your fingerprints are taken on the basis of a magistrate's warrant, the prints must be destroyed if you are acquitted or the charges are dropped. But if you give them voluntarily, there is nothing to stop the police keeping them even if you are acquitted.

Someone aged under 14 cannot be fingerprinted unless the parent or guardian consents.

Photographing
The police have no special powers to photograph you at the police station. You can refuse to be photographed — but if they photograph you anyway, there is nothing you can do except complain, although if they use force you may be able to take legal action. If you are remanded in prison before your trial, the police can apply to the magistrates' court for a warrant ordering you to be photographed.

Prevention of Terrorism Act
If you are being held under this law, the police can photograph and fingerprint you without your consent, and without getting a court order. The prints and photos will be kept after you are freed, even if you are not charged with an offence.

Identification parades
You should never agree to take part in an ID parade or any other confrontation with a witness unless you have had legal advice. You cannot be forced to take part in a parade and you should always get advice from a solicitor before taking part. If you do take part, remember:
You can have a solicitor or friend present — use this right.

You can choose your own position in the parade and change it, if you want to, after each witness has left.

You can object to any person on the parade with you or any of the arrangements made.

Bail
Always ask the police for bail when they have finished questioning you. They have the power to grant bail in less serious cases, except if you are arrested on a warrant which does not include instructions for bail. The Factsheet on Bail gives more information.

How long can I be held?
If you go voluntarily to the police station, you can leave when you want to. If you are stopped from going, this means you are under arrest.

If you are arrested WITHOUT A WARRANT the police should:

Take you to a magistrates' court within 24 hours (48 hours at weekends); or release you on bail
Release you on bail as soon as possible if the charge is not serious.

People are often held by the police for several days and it is difficult to get a lawyer to apply for HABEAS CORPUS.

Under the Prevention of Terrorism Act, you can be held up to 7 days, with the Home Secretary's consent, without being charged or taken to court.

If you are arrested with a warrant, the police should take you to a magistrates' court as soon as possible. You can only be released on bail by the police if the warrant says so. Otherwise, ask the court for bail.

In court
Do NOT plead guilty until you have talked to a lawyer.

If in doubt, plead not guilty. You can change your plea later after talking to a lawyer. You may think you're guilty, but legal advice may show that you're not or that you are guilty of a different offence.

Ask for bail. Have relatives or friends in court who can act as sureties if necessary.

Ask for legal aid. You can choose your own solicitor. In some courts, there are 'duty solicitors' available on a rota.

Summary
1. You do NOT have to answer police questions — in the street, at work, at home, at school, at the police station or anywhere else. In a few situations, you have to give your name and address.

2. If you are arrested, go quietly. Always try to remain polite and reasonable. If you have been arrested wrongly or deprived of your rights, you may be able to sue for false imprisonment or assault, or make a complaint against the police.

later.

3. If you go to the police station voluntarily, and don't want to continue the interview, see if you are free to leave.

4. Beware of any inducement or threat. Pleading guilty in return for an offer of bail can harm your case.

5. In general, don't make any statement or answer questions until you've had legal advice.

6. Ask the police for bail. If there was a warrant for your arrest, ask if it included instructions about bail.

7. Phone or telegram a friend and say where you are and which magistrates' court you are going to be taken to and when. Ask them to get a solicitor and arrange for someone to stand surety for you at court, so you can get bail. Or else contact a lawyer directly.

Read and discuss

(1) Is the law adequate as outlined?
(2) What safeguards exist?
(3) Does the individual require more protection?
(4) Do the police require more power?
(5) Are there incidents known which embody the difficulties of interpretation of the law?
(6) What are the 'Judges' Rules'?

Written work

(1) In what circumstances must fingerprints be given to the police?
(2) Can you be photographed against your will? Would photographs or fingerprints be destroyed if you were acquitted?
(3) Should you accept advice to plead guilty?
(4) Summarise your rights; use your own language as much as possible.
(5) What is meant by 'helping the police with their enquiries'?
(6) Can you be arrested without a warrant?
(7) For a minor, should a parent be present during questioning?
(8) If you felt your rights had been abused, what would you do?

Role play

Two students are selected; one poses as a suspect, the other as a policeman. Allow some time for preparation. They then enact an arrest as they think, or may have seen arrests conducted. Limit the proceedings to 5 minutes. Tape record it. The rest of the group should discuss the legal fairness of the arrest, having made notes if necessary. Play back the recording if arguments arise as to what exactly was said.

Further material: The same can be done with 'Police Questioning' and 'Search' etc. (These fact sheets are all available from the National Council for Civil Liberties.)

Topic 2   A case of murder — You, the jury

Aims

(1) To examine evidence critically.
(2) To distinguish between different kinds of evidence, statistical, scientific, subjective etc.
(3) To recognise the relevant points of both sides of an argument.
(4) To come to conclusions on the basis of evidence.
(5) To verify and defend conclusions.

Read and discuss

(1) Explain 'Judges Rules'; 'corroborative evidence'; 'rigor mortis'
(2) Were there any irregularities during arrest?
(3) Were there any irregularities during interrogation?
(4) What exactly was the evidence against the defendants?

Written work

(1) From the information you have, could guilt or innocence be proved? What exactly would need to be established?
(2) Does the case merit any complaints? How would they be phrased?

Role play

Groups of eight or more are required.
The group should be seated, preferably round a table. They should elect a foreman/woman. Discussion should develop but counter-information may need to be fed in for the sake of balance. A *full* discussion is needed so valid, adequate, defensible conclusions are reached. This must involve analysing contradictions in the information presented. If the discussion is tape recorded, crucial parts can be played back; where salient points are reached; where there are examples of people not being listened to etc.

civil liberty

National Council for Civil Liberties   186 Kings Cross Road, London WC1   Nov 1974 Vol 40 No 6

Confessions in Catford

At 1.21 am on Saturday, 22nd April 1972 the fire brigade was summoned on a routine call to 27 Doggett Road, Catford. Within eight minutes the fire was totally extinguished, but, away from the blaze in a rear room at the top of the house, firemen had found the body of Maxwell Confait – a well known homosexual, transvestite and male prostitute. He had been strangled.

Late on the following Monday afternoon, Colin Lattimore – a mentally subnormal boy of eighteen with a mental age of eight – was picked up by a panda car whilst walking down a nearby road in which he lived. He and a friend, Ronnie Leighton, were then questioned at Lewisham police station about three small fires that had been deliberately started that afternoon; by the time their parents were allowed to see them at 9.15 pm the boys had been transferred to Lee Road police station – where the Confait murder enquiry headquarters had been set up under Detective Chief Superintendent Alan Jones – and confession statements to the murder were on the point of being taken.

The statements told what appeared, at that stage, to be a convincing story laced with an impressive amount of detail. They told how Colin had slipped out of bed late on the Friday night to meet Ronnie, and how they had then broken into No 27 with the intention of stealing. They entered Confait's room and Colin strangled him when he began to struggle with Ronnie. They then set fire to the house to destroy fingerprints by sprinkling about the contents of a petrol can and setting light to it. Colin then went home whilst Ronnie went to burgle a shoe shop.

Both boys have consistently denied the truth of these statements, except while they were at Lee Road station that Monday evening. They claim that they were pressured into making a false confession and that the detail, to which they only assented, came from the police officers. They claim that they were told they would be allowed to go home if they only admitted what was put to them. Lattimore claims he was physically struck.

Although the statements were to prove to be not only completely unsupported by forensic, or even any corroborative evidence, and to be almost impossible according to the Crown's own medical evidence, they were nevertheless to prove fatal and to lead to conviction.

Unshakeable Alibi

The trial opened before Mr Justice Chapman at the Old Bailey on 1st November 1972. It was clear from the beginning that medical evidence as to the time of Confait's death was going to prove crucial. The Divisional police surgeon had estimated that the murder occurred somewhere between 8-10 pm on Friday, 21st April, whilst the Crown's pathologist thought that it could have happened anytime between 6.30-11.45 pm. If the doctors were correct, then the boys were almost certainly going to be found not guilty because Lattimore – the alleged strangler – had an unshakeable alibi. He had been during that time, for the most part, in the company of about thirty other people at the local Salvation Army youth club. The evidence was, however, to take a disastrously unexpected turn.

The prosecution in their closing address – having formally accepted Colin's alibi – invited the jury to discard the medical evidence as unreliable on the time of death, and to accept that there was a very close continuity in time between the murder and the fire at 1.10 am. In his summing-up, Mr Justice Chapman gave this suggestion further attraction by presenting

continued

the medical evidence to the jury as being a collection of 'imponderables'.

Rigour mortis normally commences within six hours of death and, by the time the fire was extinguished at 1.23 am there was evidence of rigour in Confait's body. If the boys were seriously to be said to have committed the murder between 12-1 am, then somehow this unusually rapid onset of rigour had to be explained away. Mr Justice Chapman volunteered his own explanation. The excessive heat in Confait's room, he said (actually the room was unscorched and the temperature was only 70F shortly after the fire), coupled with the alcoholic level in his body (the equivalent of 3½ pints of beer), somehow might have been able to accelerate rigour so that it appeared within about an hour of the murder.

Unscientific

It was not until February 1974, when the case had been referred to the NCCL by Lattimore's parents, that the advice of Professor Donald Teare, Britain's leading pathologist, was sought. It was only then that the wholly unscientific basis for the prosecution's suggestion, and that of Mr Justice Chapman, was exposed. Rigour mortis, Professor Teare concluded, could not have developed here within one and a half hours and the judge's implications were 'without any scientific background whatsoever'. Professor Teare was quite clear that he too would have put the time of death between 8-10 pm – well in the middle of Lattimore's alibi.

Other features of the trial were equally disturbing. One of the officers admitted in court that he had deliberately falsified his official notebook for that fateful Monday evening, the night of the questioning. Medical evidence showed that Lattimore was extremely suggestible and was prepared to agree to almost any question put to him. There was not a single piece of corroborative evidence support the alleged confessions. A statement from the wife of Confait's landlord, (a fellow transvestite who was in love with Confait), implicating her husband with the murder, was withheld from the defence lawyers and, having only accidentally come to light during the trial, cross-examination upon it was heavily restricted on the grounds of irrelevance.

Interrogation

Counsel never actually seemed to be able to convey to the jury the extreme unlikelihood of the boys being guilty of the murder on grounds of pure common sense. Perhaps though, on the evidence that was available to the defence at the time of the trial, this is not as culpable as it might seem. They were not aware that Confait enjoyed a reputation of great physical strength and could easily have handled two youthful intruders – especially Lattimore who was afraid of the dark, and Leighton who was a weak and obese fifteen year old. They were not to know that Confait's landlord and lover was to commit suicide almost two years later and that police interrogation of him in connection with the murder was to continue long after the boys' arrests. They were not to know that Lattimore's psychiatrist at Rampton, after regular and searching interviews, was later to become personally concerned that his patient was very probably innocent of the crime for which he had been convicted.

The convictions had come unanimously at 2.08 pm on Friday, 24th November 1972. On the evidence as it was presented, and in the manner that it was presented, those verdicts probably seemed acceptable enough at the time. But the Confait case now has all the ingredients for erupting into the English equivalent of the US Supreme Court's Miranda decision, and of towing in its wake an entire reappraisal of interrogation techniques in this country. The Home Office has already set up an enquiry into the landlord's suicide, and press and television interest in the case has mushroomed.

Perhaps no-one now will ever be able to prove who killed Maxwell Confait. But apportioning the guilt will hopefully not be seen by the Home Office as the sole issue raised by this disturbing case. It is only so long as the Judges' Rules are rules of practice, and thus dispensable, that it will be permissible to interview a youth with the mental age of an eight year old in the absence of a parent or another responsible adult, and then to obtain a conviction for murder on the sole basis of that interview without any corroborative evidence and in the face of expert and contradictory testimony.

Jonathan Caplan

Topic 3 We've got you taped How information about us is compiled and our means of access to it

This material is slightly more sophisticated. It poses more open-ended questions and develops a critical attitude towards the obtaining of information without knowledge or consent. Because there is a large amount of information it is necessary to be selective and it is important to follow through the implications of the material.

Aims

(1) To demonstrate comprehension of material presented.
(2) To extract relevant information from a range of sources.
(3) To collate, process, research and verify information.
(4) To develop a critical awareness of information-compilation.
(5) To attempt to determine the implications and consequences.

Initial exercise

● (1) Obtain a driving licence from a student.
(2) Write the age and sex code on the blackboard. Decode it.
(3) Discuss the implications of the code as the 'prime index' in computer terms.

Written work

Record the number of official forms you (a) have filled in, (b) will fill in in the future, (c) estimate the overall number.
Briefly write down your definition of 'privacy'.

'What the State knows about you'

Read and discuss

(1) Why are records kept in the first place?
(2) Is sophisticated data-compilation really necessary?
(3) Should we have access to any information about us?
(4) Should this be guaranteed by law?

How to crack the driver code

THE NEW COMPUTERISED driving licences were the first to carry the holder's date of birth. In what seemed a thoughtful gesture to drivers who prefer to keep their age as secret as possible, the details were recorded in a section at the bottom of the licence which, provided the dates were correct, could then be snipped off along a dotted line (subsequent licences display a row of asterisks there). But name and date of birth are the "prime index" by which the police now search their own computerised records for information which may be stored on you or your vehicle. So it was decided to retain date of birth in a thinly disguised form on every licence as part of the "driver number." The first section of the licence shown here contains the holder's abbreviated surname. The next section juggles date of birth—10/9/38 in this case; sex identification is provided in the second digit, by the simple device of adding 5 to the second digit for women (e.g. a woman born on 10/9/38 is coded 359108). The third section contains the holder's initials plus 3 symbols which, the DVLC say, are to distinguish the holder from anyone with the same name born on the same day. Although you are not at present obliged to carry your driving licence at all times, the new driver number creates the framework for a computerised national identity card. Some observers fear that it could one day include racial identifiers or codes denoting that the holder has a criminal record or is known as a political activist.

(5) Have we any guarantees that information compiled about us for one purpose will not be used for another?
(6) Compare 'What the State knows' with 'You have a right' (p. 14)
(7) Who *controls* this information?

Written work

(1) What are you guaranteed by law?
What could you do if you found out that information guaranteed
What could you do if you found out that information gathered about you was wrong?
(2) Why does the law appear to apply only to credit reference?

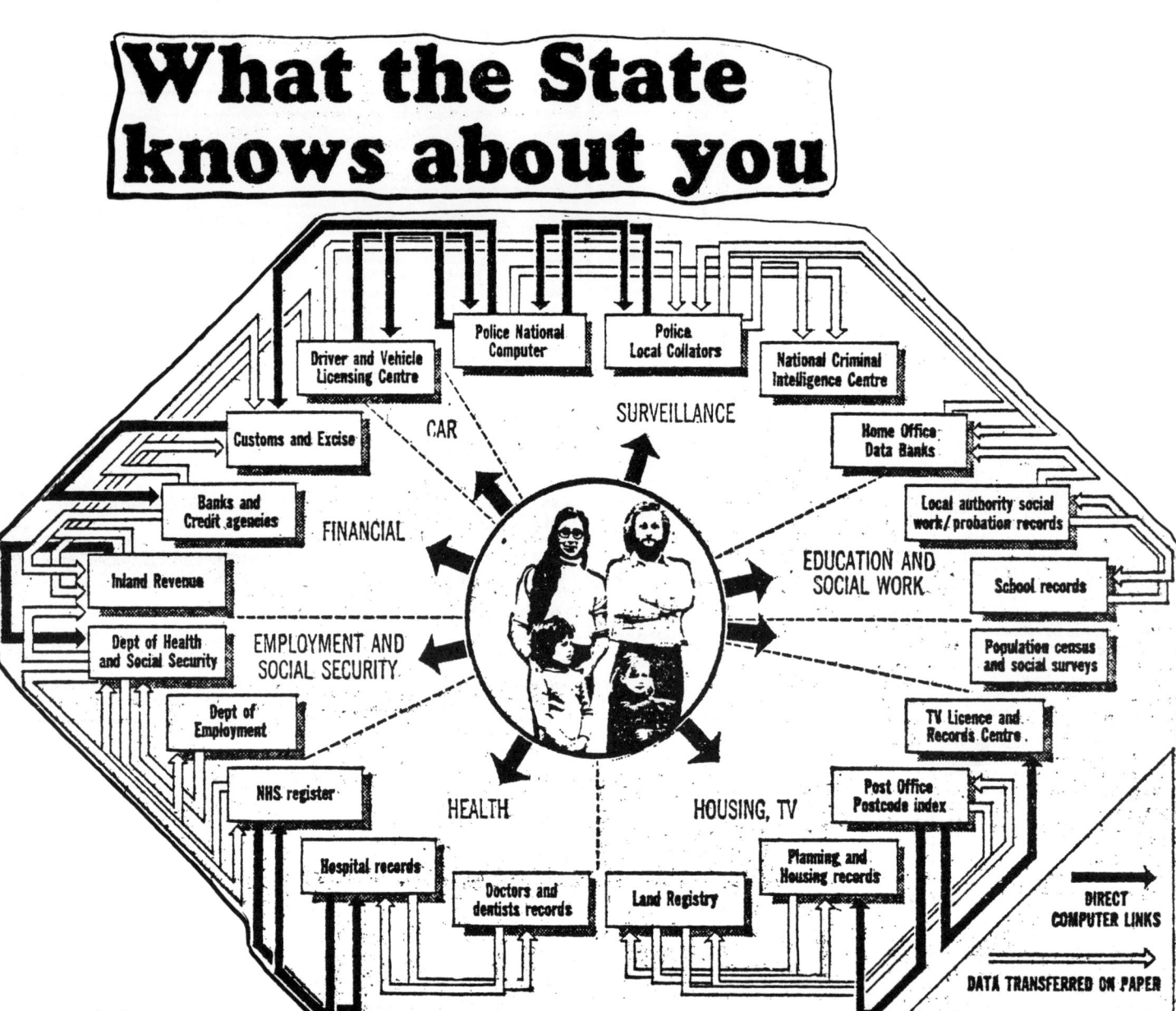

Records would look like this.
How would they influence those with access to them?

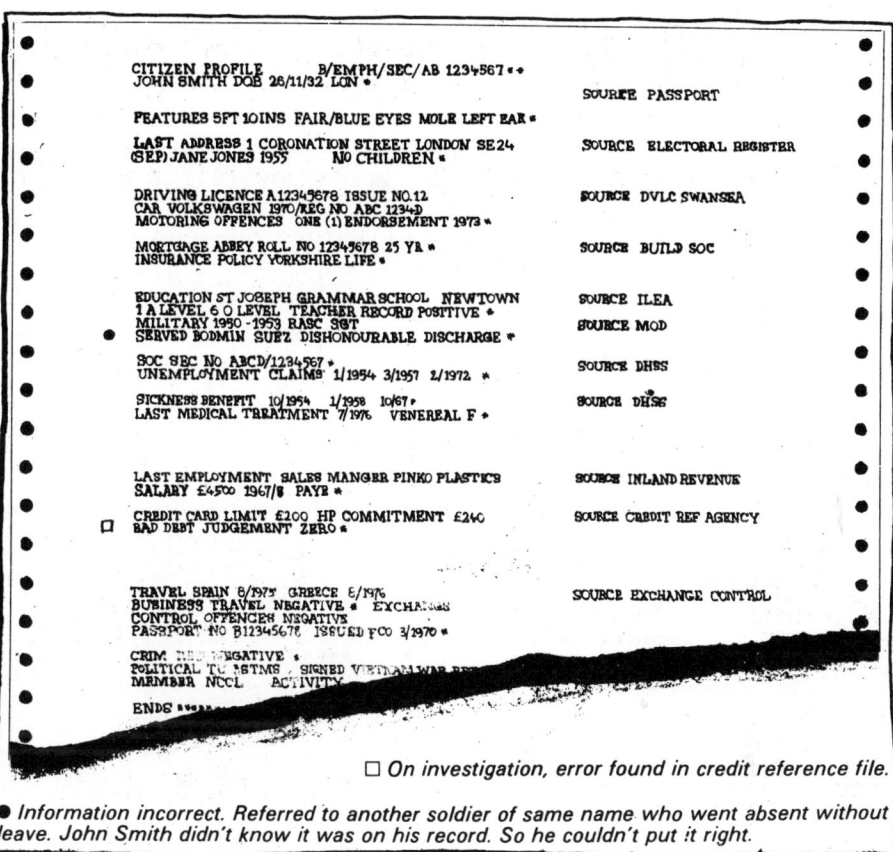

● Information incorrect. Referred to another soldier of same name who went absent without leave. John Smith didn't know it was on his record. So he couldn't put it right.

☐ On investigation, error found in credit reference file.

THIS IS THE interlocking maze of data banks and computers which knows so many of our secrets. The Police National Computer is linked to 800 police stations which can pass data to radio units within 30 seconds. National Criminal Intelligence Centre, now being completed at a secret London site, may hold up to 1.5 million files on "persons of interest." Police forces may have Local Collators; Thames Valley computerise all incoming information. Home Office Data Banks record traffic tickets, prison and parole histories; new "intelligence" systems are being developed. Recent surveys found disturbing "leakage" from Local Authority social work and probation records. Parents have no right to see and check school records. National Health Service register is mainly manual; data on every child born after 1975 is computerised. So are Hospital Records of all patients since 1970. Doctors' and dentists' records are wanted by data banks; the professions are resisting. The Department of Health and Social Security has 40 million national insurance files, computer-linked to Department of Employment records, and Inland Revenue tax files. Customs and Excise have automatic links to police national computers and to Banks and credit agencies. More than half the adult population has a computer identity code from the Driver and Vehicle Licensing Centre. Data from the last Population Census was leaked to Government departments. Post Office Postcode Index lists every house, flat and office

Sunday Times 2 June 1978

Longer written work

Compare laws concerning data-compilation in other countries with those in Britain. (Freedom of Information Act, USA, for example.)

Debate

Have a formal debate with two speakers in favour of data-compiling and two against. The rest of the group should take notes and act as a jury, coming to individually defensible conclusions.

They have got you taped

They have got your life on tape - and on file. Information about you is on records you probably don't know exist, stored away in computers and in manilla folders. The information may be correct. It may be wrong. You don't know. In most cases, you can't find out or challenge it. And you do not even know who has access to your file and all the information in it.

Who are the information gatherers?

Think of all the forms you have filled up in your lifetime. Birth certificates, marriage certificate, passport, job application, hire purchase agreements, credit cards, income tax, national census, electoral register, hospital admissions, driving licence . . . These forms are supplied by central government, local authorities, the police, employers, inland revenue, doctors, schools, credit reference agencies, building societies, insurance companies.

The information gatherers.

Yes, quite a lot is known about you. All innocent information. If it is correct. If it is not transferred from one authority to another. If it is kept confidential. If it is not abused or used for political ends.
But what if, one day, all this personal information about you, scattered in a hundred different files in a hundrdred different offices, is brought together in one computerised national information bank? What if some of the information is incorrect? And what if, as a result you are denied credit or a mortgage or a job? Imagine . . .

Who has you taped?
Why?

Are YOU in here?
Should you know?
Is the information correct?
How many people have seen it?
Legally, have you access?

SOMEBODY knows more about you than you think....

Cases from NCCL Privacy Dossier

Credit
Mr C, attemtping to expand a small, but profitable business, suddenly found himself unable to get credit. He went to the offices of a local trade association specialising in credit reports and asked for a reference on his own firm. The manager pulled out a record card and said: 'Don't deal with that bastard; he's a bad risk - people like him should be locked up'. Although the record stated that Mr C had been served with county court debt judgments over a period of three years, these judgments had in fact been made against Mr C's father, who had incurred them when he was ill and dying.

Social Security
Carol P was a separated mother claiming supplementary benefits when she saw the file kept on her by the local office. The file contained the information she had given them, but included comments and speculations about herself and her friends. It said that she was neurotic, regarded her husband as a 'father figure' and commented on her sexual relationship with her husband. The report speculated on her politics and her possible relationship with other men, including a man (described in detail) who had accompanied her to the office. The file even included the note she had left pinned to the door for a friend one day.

Job References
Mr I had been employed as a security guard for 2½ years when he resigned, fed up with the extent of petty theft in the firm. Although the personnel manager said that he would get good references, he was dismissed from his next job after two months, because his references were inadequate. He managed to get a copy of the reference, which accused him of misconduct and incompetence. Mr I's solicitor advised an action for libel. But there is no legal aid for libel, and Mr I did not have the £100 which the solicitor wanted to start the action.

Welfare records
An NSPCC inspector called one evening, when Mr X was away, and asked his wife if he could see their baby daughter. When Mr X returned from work and found out what had happened, he phoned the inspector, who said he was investigating allegations of baby-battering. Some months later, Mr X saw the file kept on them by the health visitor, which said the family had been placed on the 'at risk' register of suspected baby-batterers. He doesn't know why they are on the register and says they have never hurt the child. Mrs X is terrified that the baby will be taken away from them; Mr X is threatening to refuse to let any official see the child, so that the local authority will be forced to go to court and give evidence for their suspicions.

How does this relate to your own assessments of 'privacy'?

> **An American specialist** in government secrecy and individual privacy has defined the importance of information privacy in this way:
>
> "Power may come out of the barrel of a gun, but far more power comes out of a computer or databank, particularly if the information in it relates to people who do not know that it has been collected or cannot challenge its accuracy or use ... The definition of privacy as 'the right to control information about oneself' is therefore a good one ... The widespread collection and use of personal information is, of course, an inevitable feature of our society. The social services we regard as essential - medical, legal, social welfare, educational, credit, insurance - can only be performed when there is full and honest disclosure by the persons served to those performing the service. Unfortunately, the service providers often fail to consider the larger forces of social control whose unwitting instruments they become when they collect data from their clients. We must, therefore, constantly guard against the use of personal information as a means of exercising social control by establishing procedures to ensure that, to the maximum possible extent, people can disclose what they want about themselves only to those whom they want to tell."

You have a right......

You have a duty

You have a duty to provide some personal information, information that makes possible social and community planning, information that enables you to get a pension, claim social security benefit, have an accurate rates and tax assessment, receive decent health services and local amenities.

You have a right

But you have a right to control the personal information about you that is stored.
You have a right to challenge incomplete or irrelevant information.
You have a right to know what is known about you.
You have a right to know that information given for one purpose is not used for another.
Except for credit references, the law does not guarantee these rights.

You have a right to privacy

Nobody's life is an open book. It is not that you have anything to hide. It is simply that you have a right to a private life. A right not to be snooped on unawares, a right to shut the door when you choose.
This seclusion, this freedom from observation and probing, is called *privacy*. As life gets more competitive, more complex, more oppressive, so privacy becomes an even more essential quality of life. It is worth fighting for.

CONTRADICTIONS....

In law, you have NO right to privacy

Credit Reference Agency file of bad debtors. Now the Consumer Credit Act gives everyone the right to see their file and correct it if it is wrong.

Further information

OFFICIAL FILES store the private facts of most of our lives—addresses, hospital records, bank balances, police records, taxes paid and benefits claimed. Through a vastly complex system of interlocking computers and databanks, this confidential material can be made available to a startling range of official bodies. Yet British law allows us only minimal protection against invasion of our privacy—or wrong information on those files. PHILIP JACOBSON and DUNCAN CAMPBELL show, for the first time, how the links between the network of official databanks have been established and are being extended

NO LAW in Britain requires people to notify the police of every change of address. Yet more than fourteen million people face prosecution if they do not supply this information to a Government department, and that department promptly transfers it straight into the records of the central police computer. This curious "half-law," never formally approved by Parliament originates in the regulations governing the issue of vehicle licences.

Nothing on your application for the licence points out that some of your personal details will automatically be passed to the police. Nor is the Police National Computer the only recipient of this information. It, in turn, transfers the data directly to the Customs and Excise computer. At the same time, the computer at the Driver & Vehicle Licensing Centre in Swansea transfers data across to another machine at the Inland Revenue, and the Home Office gets the same service for following-up parking tickets. Nobody tells you that, either.

It is, of course, immensely valuable for the police to be able to punch a button and come up with a file of information on, say a driver who is a known criminal or on a suspect vehicle.

But should information supplied for one specific purpose be used for quite another—without the knowledge, let alone consent, of the person who provides it?

The present Government would appear to think not. "People asked to provide information should have a right to know for what purpose it will be used, and who is likely to have access to it," said the White Paper on Computers and Privacy which appeared at the end of 1975. "The information should not be used for a purpose other than the one for which it was given or obtained without either the consent of the person whom it concerns, or some other authorised justification."

Yet the Swansea computer is only one of a considerable number of central and local government operations which feed or

Concerned: Sir Kenneth Younger and Patricia Hewitt

are fed by other official databanks with information given by us without our permission or knowledge.

THE LAST TIME anyone counted, for the 1975 White Paper, there were 220 separate central government operations involving the use of computerised information about identifiable individuals. The list begins with " annuity payments to farmers losing land " and ends with " patient registration — hospital activity analysis and cancer registration."

The figure has certainly increased since then, and the White Paper took no account of the extensive use of computers by local authorities. Nor, for reasons which are still obscure, did it attempt to examine the scope of " non-computerised data banks " — essentially vast filing systems maintained by hand. In the private sector, a survey four years ago identified more than 2,000 computerised data banks in the insurance, banking and credit finance industries.

The practical effect is that you are, without a shadow of doubt, in a data bank somewhere. Think about how much personal information you and your family routinely provide — for the national Census; for school records; for health records; for social security and national insurance records. Every employee and every employer feeds the data banks; so does every car owner; everyone with a bank account, a credit card or an HP contract.

The impact of this mountain of personal information upon our lives depends, naturally, on how it is used.

The National Council for Civil Liberties' " Privacy Report " written by Patricia Hewitt identifies four main areas of concern:

● that information may be collected about you without your knowing or approving, by underhand or even illegal methods.

● that your file in a data bank may contain false, incomplete, outdated or irrelevant but potentially harmful material.

● that information in your file may be seen by people not authorised to do so.

● that information you give for a specific purpose may be diverted for use elsewhere without your knowledge or approval.

The potential threat to privacy is clearly the same whether data is stored in filing cabinets or inside a computer, but computers are capable of doing something which would otherwise be prohibitively expensive and time-consuming. They can pull together material from many different sources and by doing so produce what one expert calls " a new quality of information which may reveal more than the individual wishes to be known." Technically, the process is known as linkage. Those who fear the long-term implications of unifying the separate systems talk more graphically. They warn of the " Big File "—one national data bank with information on virtually every aspect of virtually every citizen's life.

If that sounds a rather farfetched vision of a technological 1984, consider the report of a US Senate committee which examined research being done at the Home Office a few years ago. " Under the direction of a central computer agency ... the technical feasibility for linking several data systems and record compatibility is being developed. This capability ... runs counter to a long established tradition of keeping separate the personal information systems maintained by major functional agencies." In the 1975 White Paper, the government emphatically denied that any plans for a central data bank existed.

What future governments may find attractive—on grounds of cost, convenience or security— is another matter. Ten years after the NCCL published the first major analysis of the threat to privacy in Britain and seven years after a committee headed by Sir Kenneth Younger produced its report on invasion of privacy, there is still scarcely any legislation framed specifically to control the operations of data banks.

Britain is, in fact, falling further and further behind most Western countries in legislating safeguards for the privacy of the individual. Most of our Common Market partners already have general laws designed to prevent the misuse of data bank information. In France, individuals have the right to check almost everything held on them in data banks; in West Germany a Data Protection Act ensures that all personal information held in computers is destroyed or permanently shelved after five years.

There is no shortage of examples for those who believe that Government data banks are already encroaching upon our privacy in important areas. Many doctors are worried about losing control over the confidences of patients once their records go into regional data banks. Private talk becomes the common property of other doctors, social workers, psychiatrists, etc. without the knowledge or consent of the patient.

The British Association of Social Workers shares the concern about confidentiality of extremely sensitive personal information obtained from clients in private interviews. One such file was subsequently read out to members of a Supplementary Benefits Commission hearing to support an official's argument that the claimant did not deserve a special needs grant. The Commission itself maintains a manual data bank of deeply personal information on some 4.5 million people; until quite recently, it was policy to discriminate against those listed in the files as habitual drunkards, homosexuals and petty thieves.

School pupils' records held by Local Education Authorities, a prime source of references for prospective employers, frequently contain judgments by teachers with which the child and parents might reasonably disagree or challenge. Only a handful of LEA's allow records to be examined.

Concern about misuse of information among the professions most directly involved is not always mirrored at government level. Before the 1971 Census, Mr William Whitelaw—then the Leader of the House—publicly guaranteed that under no circumstances would information gathered about individuals and families be released by the Census organisation to any outside body. Yet the Census organisation itself promptly conducted a follow-up survey of former nurses identified from their returns on behalf of the Department of Health & Social Security.

The computer at the National TV Licence Records office contains an index of *every address* in Britain, apparently based on the Post Office's post-code system. This data bank is used to fire off peremptory demands for immediate payment or explanation to every household without a TV licence. Should the million or so people who don't watch TV be harassed like this simply because the BBC loses several million pounds a year in unpaid licence fees?

THE NERVE CENTRE of police computer operations in Britain is housed in a small, heavily guarded block in Hendon, North London. The names of at least 24 million people are already logged in the Police National Computer's records of licensed vehicles, fingerprints, wanted or missing persons and those convicted of serious offences.

By the end of next year, it has been estimated, the PNC will contain some 36 million names— roughly equivalent to one entry for every adult in the country. Britain is considered to be one of the world's most sophisticated users of computerised data banks for police work. The results, in terms of operational efficiency and economy, have generally been satisfactory.

The issues which this raises are among the most sensitive involved in the debate about controlling data-banks, and the authorities have not improved public awareness by their grudging release of essential information. Take the 2.2 million fingerprints now held in the PNC. The White Paper says these are of "convicted persons" alone, but the present government had previously admitted that the prints also included those of people awaiting trial.

Even more important issues are raised by computerised operations which exist alongside the PNC. Very little is known about the National Criminal Intelligence Centre, beyond its broad function of keeping tracks on what the government describes as "crime, criminals and their associates and matters relating to national security."

The art of "pre-emptive policing"—anticipating crime by intelligence work—is invaluable to the community, but it has to be rigidly controlled in the public interest. What can go wrong otherwise is illustrated by a pioneer project operated by the Thames Valley Police. Nicknamed the "notebook experiment," it uses a computer to collate the vast quantity of information collected by the force's officers and previously entered in a voluminous card-index system. In the nature of police work, much of this information consists of tips from informers, unsubstantiated speculation and plain tittle-tattle.

Last April, the magazine *Police Review* revealed that a spot of idle gossip about a man's alleged sexual tastes for young boys was overheard in a village shop by a policeman's wife and found its way — via his notebook and his station's collators —into the TVP computer. It was totally untrue, yet it would have been available to any TVP officer requesting data on the man, and the allegation may have continued to damage him if he was ever subjected to a security check when applying for a job.

The Home Office, ultimately responsible for the TVP project, maintained that it had no control over the operational use of the system, and plaintively insists that there is no difference between keeping information in a card index and computerising it.

But this comment touches upon the fundamental issue underlying the use of data banks. For the threat to privacy and liberty of the individual posed by the TVP affair comes not from the computer itself, but from the unselective information gathering of the police collators. The time has surely come to respond to the recent observation of an American expert in privacy law: "The principle commodity of power in our society is information."

Sunday Times 2 June 1978

Topic 4 The Welfare State
How elements of the welfare state are treated in the media

(Note: This section can be treated as a completely separate one on Social Myth – What is Falsely Obvious.)

Aims

(1) To develop the capacity to reason effectively.
(2) To argue logically and coherently.
(3) To be aware of the underlying assumptions in an argument.
(4) To provide sources and verify information used.
(5) To examine evidence critically.
(6) To distinguish between opinion and fact; between hypothesis and conjecture; value-judgement and fact.
(7) To analyse particulars relevant to the validation of a judgement.

Initial exercise

Estimate how much you would need to earn per week to live in London independently (i.e. in a room or flat). Estimate both gross and net figures; include rent, travel, food, heating and lighting plus some social allowance.

An average can be taken for the group.

Initial discussion

(1) How easy do you think it is to get social security in this country?
(2) What are the present rates for (a) a single person, (b) a married couple with two children?

One of these questions is factual, the other speculative so don't be afraid to be outrageous. Try to remember the source of any stories you are quoting.

Visit

Before next week's class find out *exactly* what the present social security benefit rates are, preferably by having two students visit the local social security office. (Note any difficulties encountered: Are there adequate enquiry facilities? Are the necessary pamphlets available?)

Discuss

Compare with previous discussion.

'And now the truth'

Read and discuss

(1) What is the difference in circulation and readership between the two papers mentioned?
(2) Estimate how many people would read only the NoW article.
(3) What do you think is the purpose of the article?
    (Is it purely information giving?)
(4) On how many salient points do the articles differ?
(5) If Hallett had been treated unfairly, what could he do?

Written work

(1) List the differing 'facts' of each article.
(2) What is the intention of each article?

Letter writing

Write to your local paper. Find out what is the procedure if somebody feels they have been unfairly treated by the paper. (Do they have the right of reply? Has anybody ever sued the paper? etc.)

WITHOUT COMMENT

CORPORATE TAX AVOIDANCE

Programme

Michael Z. Hepker LL B LL M Barrister

Iain Stitt ACA Partner Arthur Andersen & Co.

09.30	GENERAL TAX AVOIDANCE CONSIDERAT DIVIDEND POLICY
11.00	Coffee
11.15	TECHNIQUES FOR REDUCING TAXABLE PRO
12.30	Cocktails and Lunch
14.00	SPECIAL CLASSES OF COMPANY, CLOSE GROUPS AND CONSORTIA
15.00	TAX DEFERMENT
15.30	Tea
15.45	OVERSEAS ACTIVITIES
17.00	End of Conference
	Adequate time throughout the programme has for questions.

Date: Wednesday 4th February 1976
Venue: The Inn on the Park, Park Lane, London W1
Fee: £45 inclusive of refreshments, cocktails, lunch and

—from the *Law Society Gazette*, 14 January

Socialist Worker February 1976

NEWS OF THE WORLD

Introducing the Scrounger of the Week: it takes four men's income tax to keep him

Hallett: "I'm trying for more money"

JOBLESS Charles Hallett reckons that anyone who works for less than he can get in State handouts needs his head examined.

Hallett, a 40-year-old father of five living in a council house, hasn't worked for eight years and gets £48.90 a week from the State.

It takes the income tax paid by FOUR average wage earners to find that sort of money.

But Hallett, who pays only £4.55 a fortnight in rent for his council home in Shakespeare Road, Exeter, believes in getting every penny he can out of the State—without working for it.

He says: "I think I should have more money from the State and I'm trying for it."

"If the Government can give cars to cripples why shouldn't I get more?"

The Hallett family have a TV, a record player, a tape recorder, a tumble dryer and other luxuries.

And on top of their £48.90 a week State handout — including £4.50 family allowance—Hallett told of earning £8 or £9 a week from doing electrical repair work on the side, which is paid to his wife, Priscilla, so as not to affect his dole.

Here, in his own words, is the Hallett philosophy:

❝ I wouldn't look at a job that paid less than £50 a week after deductions and without overtime.

Others can work for less than the Government will hand out if they like. More fools them. They want their heads examined.

In May the Employment Department offered to send me on a rehabilitation course to train for a job.

But when I learned I'd be paid less than the union rate during training I decided there was no point in going.

I haven't been to a job interview for over a year and have given up the idea of working.

But I think the State is very mean with its money.

I earn £8 or £9 a week repairing radios and other electrical appliances.

But, because I'm only allowed to earn £2 without affecting my unemployment payments, these earnings go in my wife's name. ❞

News of the World Reporter

AND NOW THE TRUTH

MANY READERS seeing the News of the World's article last month on 'Scrounger of the Week' Charlie Hallett must have felt their blood boil. But just look at the facts:

Charlie invited a News of the World reporter to his house in Exeter to publicise his attempt to get his eldest daughter, Prestella, out of care.

'The reporter was very sympathetic', Charlie told Fifth Column. 'He showed me the draft of the article he was going to publish, about Prestella.

'When I saw the article in the paper I just couldn't believe it. The reporter misrepresented everything I said and mentioned nothing about her.'

The News of the World claimed that Charlie gets £48.90 from the State; they also claimed that he said: 'Others can work for less than the government can hand out if they like — more fools them, they want their heads examined.'

He never said anything of the sort—and at the time of the article, he was receiving £38.40 benefit for himself, his wife and his four children.

The News of the World also failed to mention that he is an epileptic, suffering from frequent fits, and that he is on invalidity benefit, not the dole.

The critic added: 'The Hallett family have a TV, a record player, a tape recorder ... and other luxuries'.

The TV is second hand, the record player Charlie built himself, and the other 'luxuries' is a three-piece suite bought nine years ago.

Charlie has since received 12 poison pen letters. Several threatened him with physical violence, one purports to be written by six marines from Plymouth and another tells him to get back to Ireland, despite the fact that he is not even Irish.

His fits have increased as a result of these letters.

Charlie and his wife Christine have not had a holiday in seven years. A couple of weeks ago their rent went up £3 and still the council have not mended their back door, which is little more than a hole in the wall.

Their recent benefit increase has already been swallowed up by the massive increase in electricity and other prices. So much for 'scroungers'.

TIM COUSINS AND MIKE BRODERICK

'Without comment'

Read and discuss

(1) What is the purpose of the juxtaposition?
(2) What is the difference between tax avoidance and tax evasion?
(3) Who would attend such a conference? (Note the cost.)
(4) Are there moral implications in that Hallett gets £48 to feed a family (depending on which article is believed) while the one-day conference costs almost as much?
(5) Why do we hear so little about tax avoidance?
(6) Do activities of this nature not reach the front pages simply because they are legal?

Further information is now required, including

(1) How much is paid out by welfare services (including DHSS) each year.
(2) How much is illegally claimed and received.
(3) How much is unclaimed (and why).
(4) How much is illegally received in other forms, tax evasion for instance.

Tax cheating

As the table shows, a known £3.25 million was fraudulently claimed *annually* from all social security benefits—out of a total £36 million paid out *daily*. By far and away the most commonly discovered fraud was found to be amongst SB claimants—a little over £2 million. Stan Orme, the Minister for Social Security, accepts that there will be some abuse in any welfare system paying out £13,000 million annually in benefits. But he has linked this with an explanation of the range of anti-fraud measures and the extent of tax abuse.

But what puzzles the poverty lobby is the public's double morality, not only in failing to contrast welfare and tax abuse, but in the lack of concern about the underpayment of legally enforced minimum wages.

During 1976, the wages inspectors recovered almost £1 million in underpayment for low-wage earners. Yet only seven employers were prosecuted for breaching the minimum wage law. For twice the known fraud among supplementary benefit claimants, 14,488 claimants found themselves before the courts.

While much of the popular press is silent on the subject of scrooge employers (the *Daily Mirror* is the noble exception) no such ambivalence is shown about tax abuse. Revenue staff who attempt to persuade reluctant tax payers to pay up are given a rough ride by most of the press—popular and quality alike. And yet last year £27 million was recovered from detected fraud and evasion. In addition, Anthony Christopher, the General Secretary of the Inland Revenue Staff Federation, has gone on record to say that up to £500 million in taxes is lost from the self-employed alone.

Unclaimed benefits
Frank Field

Claiming a benefit to which you are not entitled always excites Fleet Street. What appears less newsworthy is the far more serious welfare "abuse" of money unclaimed by desperately poor people. In 1975, pensioners failed to pick up £65 million in supplementary pensions and other families lost £175 million in supplementary allowances. Benefits unclaimed in 1975 by the 90,000 largely single people in their parents' homes was put at £14 million.

The chart shows the total value of unclaimed supplementary benefit rising from £166 million in 1973 to £240 million in 1975 (the latest available data). In that year known social security fraud, covering all social security benefits, was £2.6 million. Put another way, for every £5,000 paid out in benefit it appears that less than £1 is wrongly claimed.

Benefits lost through claimants' fraud, 1976-77.	
	£
Family benefits	52,518
Unemployment benefit	432,521
Sickness and invalidity benefit	361,396
Maternity benefit	6,718
Widow's benefit	108,726
Retirement pension	50,934
Industrial injury	16,981
Others	4,682
Supplementary benefit	2,170,907
Total	3,205,383

As a nation we are so soft on tax abuse that large numbers of tax payers go abroad without first settling their tax bills. Last year £12.5 million was lost by those emigrating. But this is just the tip of the iceberg. Jeff Rooker MP has just discovered from the Treasury that £2,000 million tax arrears is currently outstanding, of which it is estimated only half will be recovered. The last Conservative government established an inquiry into benefit fraud. Wouldn't the most effective pre-emptive strike against the welfare bashers be to set up a similar initiative on the tax front?

New Society 16 November 1978

Unclaimed benefits total £300 M

By our Social Services Correspondent

As much as £300 millions a year is still not being claimed by the people who are entitled to it, according to Professor David Donnison, chairman of the Supplementary Benefits Commission.

"We think it is partly ignorance, partly the old problem of stigma, particularly affecting people who grew up in the days of the Poor Law, when quite deliberate stigma was attached to it." Supplementary benefit is still only reaching three out of four of those entitled to it, leaving an estimated one million people, including 600,000 pensioners, who could claim but do not.

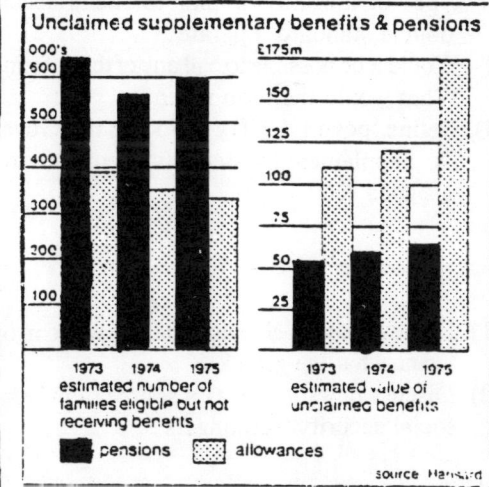

In 1974-75 the DOE estimated that 1.3 million households failed to claim a rate rebate.

What is particularly interesting about the value of non-claimed rent rebates is that it almost equals council rent arrears!

New Society 21 July 1978

Read and discuss

(1) How much is fraudulently claimed compared with what is estimated lost through tax evasion?
(2) Why does so much fraud appear to occur among those who claim Supplementary Benefits?
(3) Why is so much unclaimed?
(4) Why is so little publicity given to unclaimed benefits?
(5) What would be the effect if the NoW gave equal publicity to the unclaimed sum as it has given to Hallett's case?
(6) Do we have any choice about the type of information we receive in papers? Would readers not 'want' this type of information?

Written work

(1) Why is so little heard about (a) unclaimed benefits, (b) other types of illegality similar to social security fraud? Does a 'double standard' operate?
(2) Would it be possible to call any of this information 'propaganda'? What would the term mean?
(3) Define 'poverty'. (Try to locate the Government definition.) Do Supplementary Benefits adequately relieve it or are they designed to?

Longer written work

(1) Do newspapers give us 'what we want' in order that we grow to 'want what we get'?
(2) Discuss newspapers as a source of information on issues like social security 'scroungers'.

Visits

Go to the local employment and social security offices.
Try to get information on Supplementary Benefits and Unemployment Benefit rates.
Try to get any other information; pamphlets, leaflets etc.
Try to discreetly question any claimants there to ascertain (a) how easy they found it to understand the system of benefits, (b) whether they know their present rates of benefit and how long it will last.

Note any difficulties of access or of interpretation of information gained.

Further information for teachers

Note particularly, those aspects of the welfare state that are self-financing. Also the number of rejected claimants.

> **Frauds in City soar to record £115M**
>
> THE City of London fraud squad had difficulty coping with the £115 million worth of fraud reported 1st year, the Police Commissioner, Mr Peter Marshall said yesterday in a report.
> The number of fraud cases in the City had soared to 267, and 44 people were arrested. There was an increase of 20 per cent in the total number of offences.

This is from the *Guardian*, September 1978.
It was *not* on the front page.

Social Security

Social security payments account for about 18% of public spending. It is one area that the government will find particularly hard to cut, and on its own predictions, the proportion spent is due to rise over the next few years.

The government is committed to raising benefits, at least in money terms. This was, after all, one of the major selling points of the £6 wage freeze. 'Are the anti-inflation measures fair?... They are fair because there are provisions to help the worse off... Pensioners and people on social security will get further increases in November. £70m is to be restored to food subsidies in 1976/77 on top of what was previously planned. This will specially help elderly and low-income groups.' (*Attack on Inflation, A Policy for Survival*).

Unemployment is also going up, and shows not the faintest signs of coming down again. If the government manages to implement its proposed cuts, one major effect will be a further drastic rise in unemployment.

Pensions account for about half of all social security payments. According to the government, they will go up in line with average earnings, or prices, whichever rises faster. Until the last few months, average earnings rose faster than prices. It remains to be seen whether pensions will actually follow prices now. The £10 Christmas bonus, and cheap postage for Christmas cards, are definitely out. Other benefits, such as unemployment, sickness, maternity benefits, and supplementary benefits are supposed to go up in line with the rise in prices.

Although total spending on social security is going up, the individual recipient is by no means getting better off. For a start, increases are worked out on figures for the last six months. It is then another six months before they're given out. So benefits are always a year behind price rises. Then, the government bases its figures for price rises on the Retail Price Index. This does not adequately reflect the effects of inflation on those with low incomes. The prices of food, heating and housing are all rising faster than the average, and take a larger proportion of the income of poor families than rich.'... The inflation rate for low paid families is running at a rate of about three or four per cent faster than average, as measured by the Retail Price Index. In reality the situation is probably worse than these estimates suggest.' (Low Pay Unit. The latest round of price controls, with basic products held down to 5%, while others are allowed to soar to maintain overall profits, is an attempts to manipulate the Retail Price Index so that it fails to measure the true rate of inflation. So even if benefits keep up with the Retail Price Index, those forced to live off them get steadily poorer.

Families receiving benefits but earning a low income have an even harder time of it. Thousands of them were worse off after the last budget than before it, despite the much publicised help for the low paid said to be included in it. Family allowance increases were immediately removed in tax, Family Income Supplement taken off rent rebates. A family with two children, and an income of £30 a week, would have been 78p a week worse off after the April budget.

One particularly inhuman bit of corner cutting is the way extra needs payments are being tightened up. These payments, given for items not covered by supplementary benefits, like a new pair of shoes, or a blanket, are now harder to get than ever before. People are being made to save for items that they would previously have been able to get through extra needs payments. The total expenditure on extra needs payments was only £11½m in 1974, so the savings are minimal, the extra burden of hardship for the people involved enormous.

The unemployed, too, have a particularly tough time. Earnings-related benefit stops after 5½ months, and even the miserable flat rate ends after a year. The flat rate is £9.80 a week. Compare this to Holland where the rate is between £11 and £23.50 a day, or Germany where if you are unemployed 'for economic reasons' you get 90% of your previous pay for up to a year. Even pensioners are better off than the unemployed in this country, with a flat rate of £11.60.

The increases in social security payments don't cost the government much anyway. They are almost entirely paid for out of higher National Insurance contributions. Out of an estimated cost increase of £1,060m. for 1975/76, £910m will be paid for by the higher contributions. And as costs go up further, so will National Insurance contributions. Of all the areas of welfare spending, however, social security is one that is hardest for the government to cut.

Spending on social security benefits

Expenditure by central government in £million — 1973/4

Unemployment benefits 185
Pensions and other National benefits 3858
Supplementary benefits 730
Family Income Supplement 15
Family Allowances 359
Other benefits 312
Administration 282

Total 5741

The Supplementary Benefits Commission and how it works

WHAT does the Supplementary Benefits Commission do?

IT WAS set up in 1966 under the Supplementary Benefits Act to have a general responsibility for administrating the means-tested system of assistance.

Something like 40 per cent of claimants of State benefits get something over and above the basic scale of payments — these extras are our responsibility.

The basic rates themselves are laid down by government through parliament. The staff administering the service are civil servants at the Department of Health and Social Security.

We can give them guidance about principles, particularly over the discretionary payments, but the day-to-day administration of the scheme is a civil service responsibility.

What extra payments are involved?

THE most common is a payment for heating. The average sum is about 55p a week, but it can be £1.65 or more.

We also make one-off grants. Probably the most common is to help a mother buy clothing for her children. In other cases a family is re-housed in unfurnished accommodation and we make a grant to help them to buy furniture.

Most of our claimants have some income. Over 60 per cent are pensioners, for example.

Your benefits are supposed to prevent people suffering real hardship. How is the minimum payment arrived at and who fixes it?

THE basic rate for a married couple — say an unemployed man and his wife — is £17.75 a week, plus rent and rates. In over 99 per cent of cases we pay the whole of these two items.

For a pensioner and his wife the long-term rate is £21.45. Then there are various rates for people with dependent children.

How does the government fix this kind of poverty line? Historically what has happened is that over the last 10 or 20 years gross benefit rates have been fixed in relation to average wages.

Are they higher, or lower?

LESS. What the full total of benefit works out at will depend on your rent or rates, which in some cases is quite a large payment.

Why is it less? The Commission say

THREE MILLION pensioners, widows, disabled and unemployed get special payments from the State to help them to live. PROFESSOR DAVID DONNINSON and his seven-strong Supplementary Benefits Commission oversee the system. Donninson, 50, has a public school, Oxford University background. He has wide practical experience of administration and social security. Despite the upper-class origins, his approach is informal. He lectures businessmen on poverty at expensive luncheons dressed casually in a polo-necked sweater.

most people are on benefits through no fault of their own. But they don't get the average worker's standards of life. Are they being punished?

THE benefits are up to the level of the low-paid. Governments I think feel that they can't push benefits up to a level at which appreciable numbers of people would get more than they would get in work.

Another point that is fair to make is that if you have got more money available, it is better to put it into pension schemes or use it to give families higher child allowances and improved social insurance and lift people right off means-tested benefits. Ultimately we would like to see our scheme wither away.

What changes have you found in the pattern of benefit payments?

THE latest guidance from the Commission has been on helping people pay general fuel debts. We hope we have found a way of ensuring that people on supplementary benefits are not cut off if they have children, a sick person in the household, or if there is any reason to believe that they would be in serious hardship if they were cut off.

What about the

recent threats from the gas and electricity authorities to cut more people off?

WE had a lot of negotiations with fuel boards all over the country to get their staff to agree with our staff, to reach the position where each side knows what the rules of the game are. It has been a difficult thing to sort out.

But we can't help people who are not our claimants. Most people who are in danger of being cut off are not on supplementary benefits at all. So we haven't solved the problem.

How much more poverty is there because of the economic crisis?

WELL, there are more unemployed. The unemployed now include more and more workers with children. When unemployment was half a million or less, the majority out of work were older men, many of whom might be regarded as cases of premature retirement. They had no children, or their children were grown up.

These men are still on the dole but they have been joined by the younger worker. The Commission is worried about their needs. They may be greater because they have to have higher incomes, perhaps because of hire purchase payments, or because the way they use fuel is producing high bills.

Now one-parent families get a higher rate of payments — about 20 per cent higher — after two years. Pensioners get this higher payment from day one. But the unemployed do not. So there is a growing problem of poverty — more people may be in real hardship than we know about.

The trades unions have a vital role to play here. There is a tendency for the unions to forget people when they are cut of work.

For example, most unemployed people are allowed to drop out of unions.

Trade union officials have a lot of experience representing their members before redundancy tribunals but very little experience before supplementary benefit tribunals. There is room for a lot more work by unions in this field.

INTERVIEW BY STEPHEN JOHNS PART TWO

THE PRESS, television and radio give the impression that so-called scroungers are on the increase. Could you gives us the facts and say why there is a growing focus on 'scroungers'?

THE points I stress are that our system of benefits, the whole lot, costs £1,200m a year, only as much as tax reliefs on mortgage interest payments plus life insurance premiums.

No one gets very up tight about these payments to the better off.

The people on our system are getting very low rates of pay. The proportion of people who get more than workers in full-time jobs is very small indeed, and if they do, the reason is, in my view, because the wages of the unskilled in this country are so low.

The public are very excited about this issue in other countries besides Britain. It's partly because there is a loss of confidence in growth and partly because inflation has reduced tax thresholds and the real income level at which people start paying tax.

Some of the examples used to pillory 'scroungers' in the Press are gross distortions. What do you think about this kind of news coverage?

I FIND it very disturbing. It is cruel generally to people on social security because it attempts to make them ashamed and intimidated over something that they are getting by right.

It can be bitterly cruel to the individual family who are highlighted.

There was the case recently where a man was dubbed 'scrounger of the week' by one popular paper. After this exposure in the Press he began receiving threatening letters and the epileptic fits from which he suffered increased.

He happened not to be one of our claimants. He was on a disability pension. What this man was subject to, it seemed to me, was unprincipled and immoral journalism.

The vast majority of people are entitled to every penny they get. There are always more people not drawing the benefit they are entitled to, than those who are getting more than they are entitled to.

Sixty per cent of our claimants are for example pensioners, women over 60 and men over 65. They have a contributory pension, and in most cases we are just topping this up.

Then there are the sick, the unemployed and the one-parent families. These are the next most important groups. Among the one parent families, the biggest group are the widows, followed by the deserted or separated wives.

In all, these groups make up about 90 per cent of the claims — there are very few, if any, 'scroungers' here. Other categories are much smaller, like the students, who we only deal with during vacations.

Social security payments are a prime target for political attack by the Conservative Party and other right-wing parties. You are committed to social security and involved in running it. Are you worried

the system might be dismantled?

I DON'T think so. You mention the Conservatives. In fact the social security system fared similarly under governments of either party.

I don't think any government is going to get rid of our system or seriously injure it because it has gone on for a long time and there are a lot of people who depend utterly on it. If people die from hypothermia, or starve, the government of the day will suffer badly from these scandals.

We had the example of the Conservatives coming back with strong pressure to withdraw benefits from strikers' families.

But Keith Joseph, who was Secretary for Social Services at the time, was quite clear that we had to go on paying benefits to strikers' families.

TORIES are still demanding that payments to strikers' families be stopped. Can they do it?

IT can be done. But I think it would be a mistake. It would embitter industrial relations. I think it would encourage unions to avoid strikes, but instead to resort to go-slows and other forms of action which are even more damaging from an industrial point of view.

Workers on strike almost always feel very bitter about the way they are treated by social security.

They see it as a system hostile to their struggle, attempting to starve them back to work. What do you think about this?

FIRST I would like to comment on the bitterness. A lot depends on the industry and the union.

I observed the big miners' strike in 1974 and that went pretty well on the whole, particularly in South Wales where the union made plans in advance with the Department of Health and Social Security officers.

They in turn co-operated very well with the miners.

At one office I visited the union had got their members lined up outside. They went down the line checking if the men had got their red book, their wives' wage slip. Then they marched the whole lot through.

The DHSS staff worked right through the lunch hour and the miners came in and bought fish and chips all round.

That's the way it should work of course. But in, say, a construction workers' strike, which is badly organised and widely scattered, I'm sure it is a different matter.

Even in the well organised miners' strikes there were a lot of single men, especially youths, who got no social security and depended on their fellow workers for support. What about them?

THIS is difficult. It creates a lot of problems for the staff who know only too well the single strikers find it difficult to get by. They must have regard for this and decide how much they can give.

Why is it workers themselves do not get benefit, as of right when they are on strike?

I THINK the principle — in this country and others — is that if you are taking action which is designed to get your wages increased or conditions improved, in association with others, then you take the action.

But you cannot take it at the taxpayers' expense. I'm not arguing either way on this — but that is the principle.

What have the government spending cuts meant to the social security system?

WELL, so far we have been unaffected. Looking ahead we are bound to be affected, for example, by the decision to delay increasing child benefit allowances.

We had hoped that child allowances would have been introduced on a generous scale and that quite a number of families be lifted off our system.

But this has not happened and it has meant that some people on unemployment benefit or sickness benefits, who would have been better off on higher child allowances, have remained on our scale.

In the last deep economic slump in the 1930s benefits were slashed, a harsh means test was brought in and people were driven to desperation because private enterprise had decided that social security was a luxury that had to go. Is there a danger of this happening in this crisis?

WELL, the Commission would resign before it got as bad as something like that.

It might not stop it but we would not be prepared to administer a system that was cruel or prejudiced against the claimant.

But I don't think it's going to get that bad.

I worry about other things more, like another slow-down in improvements which would get people off means tested payments.

I would be surprised if it got as bad as the 1930s. But I have been surprised before now.

Topic 5 Forms of language within the system

Aims

(1) To demonstrate comprehension and evaluate the writing of others.
(2) To examine the adequacy of functional writing.
(3) To determine the precise tenor of a communication.
(4) To examine the relationship between form and content.

Read and discuss the 3 letters

(1) Could the benefit letter be (a) clearer, (b) shorter?
(2) What points of information need to be conveyed? Could they be conveyed in another form?
(3) What is the tone of the letters? Is the tone determined by the content? (Are they impersonal, sympathetic, jocular, ironic etc?)
(4) In the tax letter, is there any discrepancy between the form of name used in the address and the final note?
(5) Summarise the 'Dear Claimant' letter in one sentence.
(6) Do any of the letters *suggest* more than they actually say?
(7) Are there any subtextual implications?

Written work

(1) Rewrite the benefit letter as simply as possible.
(2) Write an ironic letter to the sender complaining about the simplicity of comprehension.
(3) Assume that as a married, working woman you have received the tax enquiry. Write a reply.
(4) Rewrite the 'Dear Claimant' letter in the form of a dialogue between a social security manager and a claimant. Envisage a telephone conversation with all the attendant hazards.

Longer written work

Compare the letters (or one of them) with any communications form that attempts to express meanings in a different way, preferably a poem.

In any communication please quote
590/cs

M/s D.
4 church Rd.
SW1 2QT.

Income tax

Dear Sir/Madam,

Your address is in the area covered by my office, but I cannot trace any income tax papers for you. This may be because your place of work or business is in another area or, if you work in my area, because your papers are filed by reference to your employer's name.

Will you kindly reply to the enquiries on the other side of this form and return it to me, please.

Yours faithfully,

W. R. Milton

H. M. Inspector of Taxes

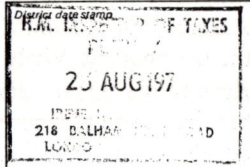

33

DEPARTMENT OF EMPLOYMENT
UNEMPLOYMENT BENEFIT OFFICE
BEECHMORE ROAD
BATTERSEA PARK ROAD
LONDON
SW11 4ES
TEL: 01 .20 911   5 SEP 7

YK 298850 C

DEAR MR ARTHURS

YOUR ENTITLEMENT TO BENEFIT IS AS FOLLOWS:-

UNEMPLOYMENT BENEFIT
FROM 22 8 77 TO 28 8 77 AT £14-70 A WEEK :: £14-70
FROM 29 8 77 TO 4 9 77 AT £23-13 A WEEK :: £23-13

YOUR CLASS 1 CONTRIBUTIONS PAID IN THE TAX YEAR ENDING 5 4 77 PRODUCED AN EARNINGS FACTOR OF £2421. THEREFORE THE INSURANCE OFFICER HAS DECIDED THAT AN EARNINGS-RELATED SUPPLEMENT IS PAYABLE WITH YOUR BENEFIT FROM 29 8 77 AT THE WEEKLY RATE OF £8-43 -

THE SUPPLEMENTARY BENEFITS COMMISSION HAVE DECIDED THAT HAD YOU BEEN PAID THE UNEMPLOYMENT BENEFIT SHOWN ABOVE BEFORE YOUR CLAIM FOR SUPPLEMENTARY ALLOWANCE WAS DECIDED, YOU WOULD NOT HAVE BEEN PAID £36.35 OF YOUR ALLOWANCE. UNDER POWERS CONTAINED IN SECTION 12(1) OF THE SUPPLEMENTARY BENEFITS ACT 1976, THIS AMOUNT HAS BEEN DEDUCTED FROM BENEFIT OTHERWISE DUE.

THE PAYMENT REPRESENTS THE AMOUNT DUE AFTER ADJUSTMENT.

YOU HAVE A RIGHT OF APPEAL TO THE SUPPLEMENTARY BENEFIT APPEALS TRIBUNAL AGAINST THE COMMISSION'S DECISION ON THE AMOUNT OF SUPPLEMENTARY ALLOWANCE WHICH WOULD NOT HAVE BEEN PAID IF NATIONAL INSURANCE BENEFIT HAD BEEN IN PAYMENT: IF YOU WISH TO APPEAL YOU SHOULD LET ANY OFFICE OF THIS DEPARTMENT KNOW WITHIN 21 DAYS.

IF YOU ARE DISSATISFIED WITH THIS, AND IN PARTICULAR IF YOU CONSIDER THAT YOUR EARNINGS FACTOR FOR THAT TAX YEAR WAS MORE THAN THAT SHOWN ABOVE, PLEASE NOTIFY THIS OFFICE AT ONCE GIVING YOUR REASONS.

YOURS SINCERELY

MRS H KING
FOR AREA BENEFIT MANAGER

Please detach here

The Post Office National Giro

pay
D Arthurs

amount under
TWO POUNDS

not negotiable

===== =====.==ONE 48

Girocheque

1 55 606 838

5 SP 77

55 £1.48

01-501

0030 UNEMPLOYMENT BENEFIT
0333 22AUG TO 4SEP 77

Paying Office Stamp

MR D Arthurs,
4 Hemel RD
LONDON
SW15 2RT

EVIDENCE OF IDENTITY MUST BE PROVIDED IF ASKED FOR BY THE PAYING OFFICER

1556068383 1556068383

76945468 C ⑈72⑈0626⑆

Dear claimant

I am now writing to you to inform you of your rates of benefit under the Social Assistance Act, 1979. As you are under pension age, you automatically come under the new short-term benefits scheme, introduced according to the supplementary benefit *Review* of July 1978.

For the next eight weeks, you and your family will receive £41.05 per week. This may seem an unduly small sum, especially as your rent in your temporary accommodation is £22, and you have four children. However, you must bear in mind the philosophy behind our new scheme. Our researches showed that two fifths of all claimants under pension age withdrew their claims after eight weeks or less. It seemed to us an extravagant use of time to go to the trouble of assessing and meeting their needs in full if they were just going to disappear like that.

Admittedly, most of them claimed again within the next eight weeks, but that just proves what unstable, impoverished, needy people they were. Our whole administrative system is terribly complicated, with literally dozens of staff working on any one claim. It is wasteful of our staff's time if claimants' circumstances keep changing, especially if they are in urgent need.

You must appreciate that it is an essential feature of the new scheme that the rates of benefit are absolutely standard, and the same for every claimant, whatever his circumstances. This seems only fair, even though it is not the way we treat longer-term claimants. You may consider that £8.40 is rather a low amount to include as rent, as your particular rent is somewhat higher than this. But it would entirely destroy the essential simplicity of the scheme if we started to make adjustments for individual circumstances. In your own case, we can only advise that you and your family make some kind of decision whether to eat or pay the rent.

At the end of eight weeks, if you are still alive, and still wish to claim, you will be re-assessed, and transferred to a completely different scale of benefits. You may wonder what is simpler about a scheme which involves two assessments, on different scales.

But I can assure you that, even though the number of questions we have to ask claimants is just as many in each assessment, and they all have to be asked twice, the new rules for short-term claims are far easier for *our staff* to understand. We are trying to relieve them of the immediate strain of having to deal with very poor people.

If you find these new rules confusing and unfair, do not hesitate to write again to us, but you can be assured that there is nothing you can do about them.

This is the second in a series of "imaginary letters" by Bill Jordan, stemming from the recent SBC *Review.*

New Society September 1978

Subject area: Social relations

The social structure of which the student is a part and the role he or she plays in it; interpersonal relations.

Aims

(1) To extract and interpret relevant information from a range of sources (visual, statistical etc.).
(2) To locate and analyse sources of reference.
(3) To determine the consequences of a communication.
(4) To identify concepts of cause and consequence.
(5) To identify issues leading to acceptance or rejection of certain attitudes.

Initial writing exercise

(1) 'After his exams at the end of his first year at medical school, John found himself at the top of the class....'
(2) 'After her exams at the end of her first year at medical school, Anne found herself at the top of the class....'

● Divide these as evenly as possible between the students.
They should complete the *careers* of John and Anne in a maximum of ten sentences. (Students should not know that they have different stories.)

Analyse and discuss the results including

(1) Any different expectations between John and Anne solely due to sex difference?
(2) Does Anne suffer any resentment not accorded to John?
(3) Does Anne's career (if that is the case) end at marriage? (Pay particular attention to whatever happens to Anne after her children (if any) have grown up.)

Topic 1 'Am I an Image?'

Read and discuss

(1) In what capacity do women exist in the cartoons and the advertisements?
(2) What are the assumptions behind the cartoons?
(3) Why doesn't the girl in the '*Mirror*' cartoon walk away?

(4) What are the songs suggesting women should be?
(5) Do you know of any songs or images which contradict these images?
(6) What is meant by 'feminism'?
(7) What are the implications of the feminist statement?

MEN ONLY
by Michael Heath

'YOU know women they're all the same, as soon as we got married I told her straight, I said, I go out to work an' you look after the house. I'll see you all right, but if I want to go out with the lads for a few jars I'm going and I don't want any nonsense my girl. Anyway she doesn't like football so she's not missin' nothin'... No she's not at home now she left me didn't she the selfish....'

"She's no conversationalist—I've tried every subject from gear-boxes to sparking-plugs!"

I had to let it happen....
(*from 'Don't cry for me Argentina'*)

The central conundrum left unsolved by psychoanalysis is what do women want.... from men. (*Sigmund Freud*)

You'd better watch out baby
Here comes your master
                (*Jimi Hendrix*)

Every woman should be
What her man wants her to be
                (*Marvin Gaye*)

What is it, I'll rape it
                (*The Who*)

Take good care of my baby
And if you should discover
That you don't really love her
Then send my baby back home to me
                (*Bobby Vee*)

My, my; it's a full life between the dressing table and the bed.
(*Feminist comment*)

Bentalls can save you giving your wife some help around the house

Adman's woman: from the *Daily Mail*.

SOCIAL RELATIONS 33

Overheard

Why do men always refer to women who seek equality as 'underwear incendiarists'?

When God invented man, she was only testing.

Woman to barman: Two pints, please.
Barman   : We only serve men here.
Woman   : In that case, we'll have two as long as they don't look like you!

Q. Should women have equal pay for equal work?
A. Why the hell not. They've proved their equality twice this century already!
(Written reply by TEC year 1 student.)

Cartoon by Mel Calman, from "The Framing of the Female," by Pat Barr.

Koppers Football Team (women who built coke ovens).

Read and discuss

Compare the images and 'overheards'.

Written work

(1) See how many images you can locate of women 'hidden from history' (like the football team). Note if they are any more difficult to locate than 'conventional' images.
(2) Locate two pieces of writing about women, one by a feminist and one other. Compare and contrast them.
(3) Examine the images of women (not only the advertisements) in your local paper. Are the women portrayed in a patronising way or equally?

Research

Interview a female lecturer in your college. Concentrate on (a) discrimination, (b) career/family choice.

Topic 2a Women's work and apprenticeships

Read and discuss

(1) Why are the majority of women in these occupations?
(2) Why are so few in the professions?
(3) Do women really have equal *opportunities*?
(4) Is certain work (unskilled, low-paid) seen as 'women's work'? Why?
(5) Does this make women more dependent on men, both in terms of marriage and economically?
(6) Can you spot the woman in the picture? Why are all the men dressed in women's clothing?
(7) Why do fewer men than women do apprenticeships in hairdressing?
(8) Any differences between the expectations of a brother and a sister in your family.
(9) Any differences in the expectations of parents for them.
(10) What can be done to encourage both men and women to try new subjects? (in schools)

Written exercises

(1) Why are more married women now working?
(2) Is it only because women now have less children that they go back to work?
(3) *Men*: Speculate on whether you will both work if you get married.
(4) *Women*: If you get married/have children will you go back to work afterwards?

Longer written work

(1) Are laws needed to effect change or something deeper, more fundamental?
(2) What real choices of career/children does society provide for women?

Role play

Set up an interviewing panel for a job as an apprentice engineer. Interview both a man and a woman.
Note any difference in questions and attitude specifically due to sex differences.

Research

Find out how many women apprentices in your college are doing (a) engineering, and (b) hairdressing/secretarial. Interview a number. Compare wages, conditions etc. Would any/many have preferred a different apprenticeship. Why? How did they come to be in this particular one?

Apprenticeship

On leaving school, educational and training inequalities multiply. In 1974, 43% of boys entering employment went into apprenticeships, but only 6% of girls — and the vast majority of these are in hairdressing. Indeed, the Department of Employment Gazette, in its article 'Recent Trends in Apprenticeship Training' considered the number of girls receiving apprenticeships so insignificant that it restricted itself to 'changes as reflected in the figures for boys' (DE Gazette, November 1975). In 1970 there were 110 women apprenticeships to skilled craft occupations and 112,000 men. The situation has not changed radically since.

Day release schemes are designed to continue the general education of those young people who leave school at the minimum leaving age and to enable them to overcome some of the consequential disadvantages. The last set of figures compiled was for 1971, and they are no longer collected. These showed that 35.9% of male workers under 18 were given day release education, and only 9.6% of women workers.

While 10.5% of girls go on to higher education compared to 12% of boys, boys outnumber girls two to one at university, while four times as many girls as boys go to teacher training college. The fact that this is largely a matter of self-selection, far fewer girls *apply* to university, shows how effective the conditioning process is.

The employment boys and girls get on leaving school reflects the bias in their education.

Type of employment	Girls	Boys
Apprenticeships	6%	43%
Leading to professional qualification	2%	1%
Clerical	40%	7%
With planned training	17%	17%
Other	34%	32%

And what are the chances of getting retrained? Much has been heard of the government's Training Opportunities Scheme, designed to retrain sections of the workforce in conditions of high unemployment. At the government-run Skillcentres, where courses are run in skilled crafts, of the 12,074 people in training last December, only *32* were women. The reason given, that the courses are for jobs traditionally done by men, only shows the scale of the problem, and how little this government, for all its rhetoric of equality of opportunity, is doing to overcome it. Of the 14,356 women reciving government training under the TOPS scheme (40% of the total), the vast majority were studying commercial and secretarial subjects. The reality of most office jobs is that they are poorly paid, repetitive, and offer little hope of promotion. In 1975, half of all women office workers earned less than £31.86 gross a week.

But the war did bring one lasting benefit. It destroyed the last shreds of the view that women were not responsible enough to have the vote. A 1918 bill gave the vote to about half of all eligible women, and by 1928 all women had the vote on the same terms as men. Thus ended more than 50 years of bitter, and sometimes violent, struggle.

The coming of the second war saw women once again needed in the factories as the men went off to war. (Indeed it was not only the men who went this time. Some anti-aircraft batteries were run by women: the first time that the female role in the armed forces had included the opportunity to kill.) Indeed, so great was the demand for women's labour that more and more *married* women found themselves working. As a result something had to be done to provide childcare facilities so that the children could be looked after while their mothers were at work. There was a big expansion of nurseries, and of school-meal services.

Nursery provision was cut back after the war (there are still far too few places to meet the demand) but, from then on, married women did start to enter the workforce in increasing numbers. Indeed in the full employment years of the affluent 1950s and 1960s, women were the only untapped source of labour available. By 1951, about a quarter of all married women were working, compared with a tenth 20 years before. And last year (1977), it was estimated that, for the first time, the proportion of all married women either working or looking for work would reach a half.

A lot of these are older women. Earlier marriage, smaller families (helped by the spread of efficient contraception), and longer life expectation have combined to give married women a far longer period after childrearing has ended. Only 100 years ago it was common for women to have only three or four years from the end of their childrearing period to their own death. Today the equivalent period may be as long as 40 years. This has left the older married woman free to join the labour force.

And it is not only mothers who have ended their childrearing phase who are working. An increasing proportion of women with dependent children are working too. In 1961, less than 25 per cent of married women with two or more dependent children were in the workforce. By 1971, this had risen to nearly 35 per cent, and the indications are that the rise has continued since then.

On the face of it, this does seem to suggest that the idea that woman's place is in the home is beginning to weaken. Of course many working wives do only part-time jobs, which can be fitted in with childcare: there does not seem to be much change in the view that looking after children is essentially a female task. Nevertheless, more women are working outside the home, and bringing back their own pay packet.

What the effects of this are likely to be can only be guessed. Michael Young and Peter Willmott in *The Symmetrical Family* (1973) suggest it may lead to greater equality in the home, with less rigid divisions between sex roles, and with greater economic independence bringing women higher social standing.

But the women's movement itself is arguing quite the opposite case: that the world of 1978 is still a world where women take second place. There is plenty of evidence for this view. An example was given recently by the Labour Research Department which looked at the 20 biggest firms in Britain and found that of their 288 board members not one was a woman.

New Society

Why are girls more likely to be doing English or Domestic Science, and boys doing Chemistry or Technical Drawing? It is not because the 'arts' are easier than the sciences. Nor is it because girls aren't as clever as boys. In fact, girls have a better pass rate than boys in CSEs, O-levels **and** A-levels!

Boys and girls follow very different paths when they leave school too. Some go on to further and higher education. If you're a boy you are at least twice as likely as a girl to get to university.

Full-time students at universities in 1974

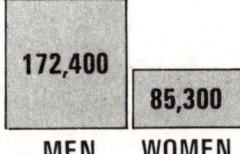

172,400 MEN 85,300 WOMEN

These two diagrams show what happens to both boys and girls who do find jobs (1974 figures):

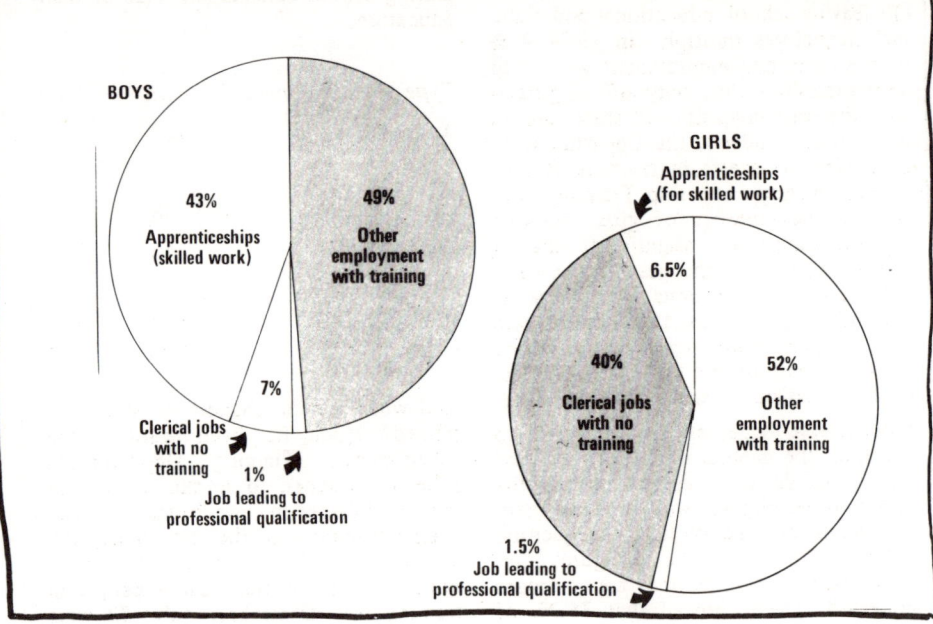

BOYS
- 43% Apprenticeships (skilled work)
- 49% Other employment with training
- 7% Clerical jobs with no training
- 1% Job leading to professional qualification

GIRLS
- Apprenticeships (for skilled work) 6.5%
- 40% Clerical jobs with no training
- 52% Other employment with training
- 1.5% Job leading to professional qualification

All Virago Ltd

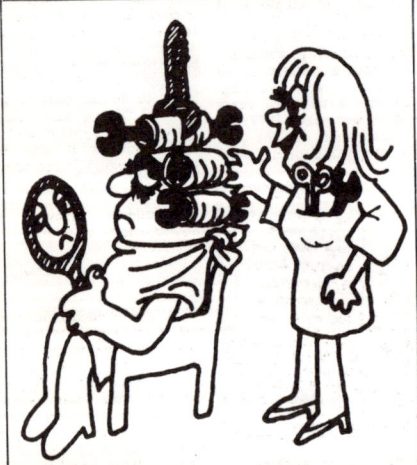

"I really wanted to be a mechanic, but there were no apprenticeships for women!"

More girls than boys go to colleges of technology and polytechnics. But the girls take mainly clerical or catering courses, while most boys do science-based vocational courses. Day-release schemes at colleges are attended by nearly 4 times as many boys between the ages of 16 and 18 as girls.

Day-Release Students, November 1974

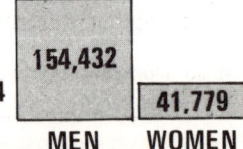

154,432 MEN 41,779 WOMEN

In teacher training colleges, female students outnumber males by 3 to 1. But what happens to them? Most head teachers in primary and secondary schools are men. And there are six times as many men teaching full-time in further education colleges as women.

SOCIAL RELATIONS 37

Out of the small number of girls who do apprenticeships, the vast majority of them are in the suitably 'feminine' jobs of hairdressing and manicure.

The Sex Discrimination Act should be evening things out by now. But it will take years of re-education for ALL those involved — employers, parents teachers, boys and girls themselves — to come round to the view that education, training and opportunities are not 'wasted' on girls.

2 Here are 3 possible reasons why so few girls do science subjects for exams. How far do you agree with each one?
a) not enough money is spent on science facilities at girls' schools.
b) girls know they won't be able to use science qualifications in later life.
c) Ideas of what's feminine from TV, films, teachers and parents stop girls choosing science.

The school-leavers who go straight into employment are even more sharply divided by sex than students. (An increasing number of school-leavers are going straight into unemployment, too. Even then, girls have fewer opportunities than boys. In 1977, only a quarter of the young people on Job Creation schemes were girls).

DID YOU KNOW

THAT FOR EVERY **1 GIRL** WHO DOES **PHYSICS** FOR-CSE
▲
THERE ARE **7.4 BOYS?**
●●●●●●●◖
AND FOR EVERY **1 GIRL** DOING **TECHNICAL DRAWING**
▲
THERE ARE **78.4 BOYS?**
●●◖

BUT IT'S THE OTHER WAY ROUND IN **DOMESTIC SCIENCE**,
WHERE THERE ARE
12.3 GIRLS
▲▲▲▲▲▲▲▲▲▲▲▲◣
FOR EVERY **1 BOY.**
●

AND IN **COMMERCE**, THERE ARE **3.8 GIRLS**
▲▲▲▴
FOR EVERY **1 BOY.**
●

WHY?

Women's Work
Nearly eight out of ten adult employed women work in one of four types of job:

Main Occupations of Women	Percentage of all employed adult women
Office & communications	30.3 %
Catering, domestic etc services	20.4 %
Unskilled and semi-skilled production	15.9 %
Sales	10.1 %
	76.7 %

Source: New Earnings Survey 1972, Department of Employment.

Training for School-Leavers, 1972
The table shows the numbers, to the nearest 500, of school-leavers taking up courses. The total number of school-leavers going into jobs in 1972 was 259,000 boys and 228,000 girls.

	Apprenticeships: in manufacturing industries	Apprenticeships: in non-manufacturing industries	Full-time & similar courses	Sandwich courses	Day release
Girls	1,000	17,000*	118,000	5,500	9,000
Boys	32,500	68,000	144,000	36,500	473,000

* 14,000 of these apprenticeships were in hairdressing and manicure.
Source: Department of Employment and Department of Education and Science.

Women's average weekly earnings as a percentage of men's — full time manual

1950	1955	1960	1965	1970	1971	1972	1973	1974	1975
58.7	51.7	51.1	49.0	49.9	51.1	51.1	51.7	55.5	57.4

(Department of Employment)

SOCIAL RELATIONS

Woman in a crowd: outnumbered, but fighting back

The law, with its wigs, waistcoats, and old-world courtesy, is still a masculine club. It tolerates women, but does not encourage them. Times are changing slowly but it will take a few brilliant individuals to break down old prejudices

The case of the missing sisters in law

Guardian 6 December 1977

Most of the jobs undertaken by women are classed as low-grade, although many require a high degree of skill. About two thirds are classed as non-manual and the majority of these are such occupations as clerks, typists, shop assistants, etc. An enquiry into the type of work performed by women in manufacturing industry was carried out in 1968 for the Ministry of Labour. This showed that 29 per cent of employees in manufacturing were women—but that they were in the main employed only in less skilled and less responsible areas. Thus women formed 91 per cent of canteen staff, 62 per cent of clerical and office staff, but only 5 per cent of skilled production workers, 1 per cent of skilled maintenance workers and 4 per cent of managers and superintendents.*

The opportunities for girls to train for skilled jobs are far fewer than for boys. A government Social Survey of Women's Employment found that in 1965 less than 1 in 20 types of work undertaken by women required training lasting more than 6 months.

In 1972, only 7.9 per cent of girls entering employment for the first time went into apprenticeships for skilled occupations, as against 38.8 per cent of boys. And even amongst these few girls, numbering 18,000 in all, nearly 14,000 entered apprenticeships for hairdressing and only 814 obtained apprenticeships in the whole of manufacturing industry. In contrast, there were 32,293 apprenticeships for boys in manufacturing.

Women university students are outnumbered by men by two to one, although girls do just as well at school as boys. In 1968 women accounted for only 8 per cent of the total numbers in the higher professions, as against 6 per cent in 1921—a slow rate of progress. Only one in every 11,000 professionally qualified engineers is a woman; only 6 per cent of barristers are women, and there is one woman High Court judge. Women have about 8 per cent of the most senior jobs in government departments, ie of the administrative class of the Civil Service. Only 26 women MPs were elected to the House of Commons in 1970—the same number as in 1966—out of a total of 630 MPs. The present Tory Government has one woman Cabinet Minister, while the previous Labour Government had two.

PM calls for closer links between education and manufacturing

Callaghan tells industry to bring on the girls

By Michael White, Political Staff

The Prime Minister yesterday combined a plea for greater recognition of the importance of manufacturing in Britain with an appeal for more girls to break through the "traditional barriers or stereotypes which effectively restrict industry's recruitment to half our school-leavers."

Mr Callaghan, who was addressing the National Union of Teachers' careers convention in North London, stressed the themes he has been hammering at in the year since his "great debate" speech at Ruskin College, Oxford.

Guardian 28 October 1977

Call for more girl engineers

ONLY ONE woman in 500 is an engineer in Britain, the conference of the Girls' Schools Association was told in London yesterday.

In Europe the figure is one in 60. In the United States it is one in 50. In Russia it is one in five. And in China it is one in three. Yet Britain badly needs more engineers. Even discounting the factors of state encouragement and of the sheer economic necessity for mothers to work in the two Communist countries, the discrepancy between Britain, Europe, and America was explained in two words—"sex stereotyping."

Miss Dorothy Dakins, head of Red Maids School, Bristol, and chairman of the Independent Schools Information Service, said that it began in the cradle.

Dr Ewen McEwen, vice-chairman (engineering) of Joseph Lucas, said that co-education was making it worse. "The boys tell the girls that maths is for boys—and the girls are channelled into cookery."

Mr McEwen disclosed that a pioneer scheme run by the Engineering Industries Training Board to prepare girl school-leavers for technician work was arousing "serious worries" about its future at Lucas's because fewer than 100 girls had applied.

"I am afraid that careers teachers have been advising girls away from these opportunities into the safer, cosier world of banking, insurance, retailing and secretarial work. I have made a particular study of women in professional engineering and am much struck by the femininity of those who have succeeded. Talent is not sex-linked.

"Let us immediately dispense with the myth that men in industry are generally using great physical strength unavailable to women. The fact is that in making, say, gear wheels, the very small are lifted by hand and the very large have to be lifted mechanically.

The changeover point has been going down in weight all my working life, with a very proper reduction in hernias and back injuries. There is absolutely no reason why the use of mechanical aids cannot be applied at a weight which makes the work light enough for any girl."

WHO NEEDS YOU BABY?

'Bring on the girls'

Read and discuss

(1) Can women simply 'break through' as Mr Callaghan is suggesting?
(2) Are fewer people going into engineering?
(3) Is more positive discrimination required for women?

'More girl engineers'

Read and discuss

(1) What is meant by the term 'femininity'?
(2) Is the 'retention of femininity' the best argument for getting more women into engineering. (Are items like pay and conditions not more important?)

Project

Write letters inviting a man and a woman doing jobs unusual for their sex to come and talk to your group.

Research

Local engineering firms.
Do they provide (a) creche facilities, (b) equal opportunities, (c) equal pay for equal work?

Design

(1) Design an advertisement to attract more women into engineering. Should the basis of its appeal be any different than if it was aimed at men?
(2) Design an advertisement aimed at men to persuade them that women can be engineers, too.

Topic 2b   Equal pay and the law

Read and discuss

(1) How effective are claims for equal pay at industrial tribunals?
(2) In 'attack on high cost...', why was the employer prepared to pay such high legal fees in order to contest the equal pay claim?
(3) Are there financial disincentives for employers as regards equal pay for women?
(4) Speculate on differences between equal pay and equal opportunities.
(5) Do tribunals offer encouragement to women seeking equal pay?
(6) In recognition of previous discrimination, should there now be positive discrimination in favour of women?

Written work

(1) *Information Retrieval*: Bring the figures up to date.
(2) Speculate on positive discrimination. Should its form be merely economic?
(3) (Or role play) Comment on Cases A and B.
How successful would each be?

Visit

Arrange a visit to a hearing of an equal pay claim at an industrial tribunal. Write up what happened from notes taken during the proceedings.

THE SEX DISCRIMINATION ACT

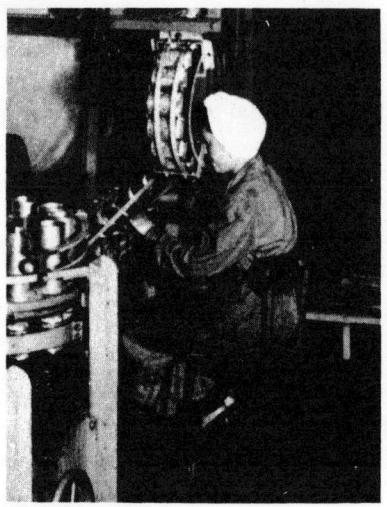

Canning at 200 a minute.

Equal pay claim fails

A WOMAN who checked the work of quantity surveyors was paid less than a labourer, an industrial tribunal heard yesterday. But Mrs Violet Pittam lost her claim before the Birmingham tribunal for equal pay with the lowest paid men who work with her at the Royal Ordnance Depot, Bicester.

The tribunal backed a system which fixed her wages as a percentage of a labourer's wage and said that she could only claim equal pay if she could show that a man doing the same job as her was getting more money. No one was doing exactly the same work.

Guardian

Equal pay claim rejected

Mrs Ann Hunt, aged 21, has lost her court fight for equal pay. An industrial tribunal in Birmingham yesterday rejected her claim—the first under the new Equal Pay Act—for the same salary as a man doing a similar job.

Mrs Hunt gets £2,016 a year as a wallpaper stock controller at Crown Decorative Products in Halesowen, Worcestershire—£481 less than paint stock controller, Mr John Fletcher, aged 28.

The three-man tribunal ruled that the gap between their salaries was genuinely due to material differences in their work. Mrs Hunt, of Beech Street, Halesowen, said she was disappointed by the decision but added: "It was worth going through with."

Her only other regret was that the case had strained relations between herself and Mr Fletcher, with whom she shared an office. "He doesn't talk to me now but I can stand it. My relations with the management are very good." The tribunal, in a written judgment, said that Mrs Hunt's outlook was coloured by a firm and settled belief that everyone in the same grade should get the same pay.

FIRST LADY: Mrs Ann Hunt, 21, who yesterday became the first woman in Britain to take her equal pay fight to court, over a claim that a man doing the same job in a wallpaper factory earns more than her

Guardian

the legislation requires the complainant to prove that she or he is being discriminated against on the grounds of sex, and not for any other 'material difference' (for the widespread nature of 'material differences', and the ease with which employers can find them, see the section on Tribunal Judgements in Equal Pay Cases). Perhaps the ineffectiveness of such a law is most easily demonstrated by looking at the results of the Sex Disqualification (Removal) Act of 1919. This made it illegal to discriminate against women entering professions. Fifty years and more after, only 4% of architects are women, 8% of barristers, 1% of chartered accountants, 0.07% of managers in manufacturing industry. The Act may well be important in terms of women's expectations, but there is little real hope of it changing women's role in society until women themselves organise consciously to do so — and in that situation the existence or otherwise of legislation is going to make little difference.

C/S Special Report: *Women*

Attack on high cost of equal pay cases

An Appeal Court judge in London yesterday protested at the costly legal complications that had developed in deciding cases under the equal pay laws. The court's decision to grant a woman clerk another £5.54p a week to bring her into line with a man doing the same job, will involve the employers, Clay Cross (Quarry Service), Ltd, of Cheadle, Staffordshire, in costs which could exceed £2,000.

To decide the case, the appeal judges had to consider decisions that included two of the Employment Appeals Tribunal, six of the United States Federal Courts, two of the United States Supreme Court, two of the European Economic Community Court, Article 119 of the Treaty of Rome, and a Community Council Direction.

"I found all these complications disturbing," said Lord Justice Lawton. "Parliament intended that industrial tribunals should provide a quick and cheap remedy for what it had decided were injustices in the employment sphere. The procedure was to be such that both employers and employees could present their case without having to go to lawyers for help."

But what had happened in this case was that for 2½ days the Appeal Court had heard "excellent displays of legal learning" over the construction of a four-line sub-section of the Equal Pay Act. "If the wording of the relevant statutes has opened the door to legal subtleties, there is nothing the courts can do to stop what I regard as an unfortunate development," said the appeal judge. "The remedy lies with Parliament."

Lord Justice Lawton was giving judgment allowing an appeal by a 22-year-old sales clerk, Mrs Karen Fletcher, of Tean Road, Cheadle, who claimed she was entitled to be paid the same as a man, aged 24, doing the same work.

Guardian 12 July 1978

New court ruling on equal pay

TRIVIAL job differences cannot be an excuse for not paying women the same as men doing comparable work.

This grudging step forward towards equal pay for women was conceded yesterday by the president of the Employment Appeal Tribunal, Mr Justice Phillips.

He said industrial tribunals must take a broad view when considering claims under the Equal Pay Act.

Phillips made his comments while giving the Appeal Tribunal's (EAT) reasons for upholding an equal pay award to a Yorkshire cook Mrs Barbara Lawton.

She does the directors lunches in a separate dining room at the Capper Pass Ltd works in North Ferriby.

The firm paid her less than two male assistant chefs who cook in the factory canteen.

Mrs Lawton won her claim to an industrial tribunal for equal pay. The directors appealed to the EAT to overturn the verdict.

It was the first case under the Act to come before the Appeal Tribunal.

In explaining the ruling in favour of Mrs Lawton, Justice Phillips said that industrial tribunals should not be required to make too minute an examination of 'like work'.

If differences between jobs were 'insubstantial', they should be disregarded, he added.

The only differences which will prevent work which is of a broadly similar nature from being "like work" are differences which in practice will be reflected in the terms and conditions of employment, Phillips concluded.

Guardian 20 October 1976

EQUAL PAY AND THE LAW

The Equal Pay Act covers the pay and conditions of workers. Though clearly aimed at women's pay problems, the Act applies equally to men. Under the Act an individual woman worker is entitled to equal treatment with a man when she is employed on *like work* to that of a man; or on a job *rated of equal value* under job evaluation. An employer will be within the law if he can show that any unequal treatment is the result of a *material difference* (other than the difference of sex) between the woman's case and the man's.

The Act establishes a woman's right to *equal treatment* on the terms of her contract of employment when she is employed:

(1) on work of the *same or broadly similar* nature to that of a man; or
(2) in a job which, though not the same as the man's, has been given an *equal value* to the man's job under job evaluation.

The question of what exactly is equal treatment is obviously crucial. The Act does not say that treatment must be identical; it states that a woman's terms of contract must be *not less favourable* than the man's. Women who consider they have a claim under the Equal Pay Act (EQPA) or the Sex Discrimination Act (SDA) can take their complaint to an industrial tribunal. (In this article we look at six of the cases that have been brought.) Of the applications to tribunals under both Acts in the first half of the year, over 60 per cent were withdrawn by the applicants before they got to a hearing. A huge majority of the applications being made fall under the heading of the EQPA – less than 4 per cent were concerned with the SDA. Most of the cases that do get to tribunals are lost: 72 per cent of EQPA applications and 73 per cent of SDA applications were dismissed in the period for which we have figures (roughly the first six months in the life of the two new Acts).

Case 1 Ms Marchant was one of 20 Clock Assemblers in the Alarm Clock Assembly Department at Metamec in Cambridge. She claimed like work and equal pay with the five men in her section who were classified as journeymen and called Electric/Alarm Movement Inspector/Rectifiers. They were paid £52·84 basic and the women £47·82. The tribunal concluded that the jobs did not involve like work because the men were able to do minor repairs (as distinct from very minor repairs in the case of the women). It was also agreed that the men could (if necessary) do major repairs. The company claimed that the men's training involved three weeks off the job and two weeks on: Ms Marchant told the tribunal her job took "a couple of days to pick up". But neither she, nor the union official with her, knew what training the men had. Ms Marchant also claimed, on her application form, under the Sex Discrimination Act, that the company had denied her access to be transferred or promoted to journeyman, and refused or omitted to offer her that status. This claim was dismissed by the tribunal because there was no evidence. The company said no jobs had become vacant in the period, furthermore Ms Marchant agreed she had not applied for a new job or for promotion or transfer. (COIT 491/213)

A tribunal has to dismiss a case where no evidence is available to substantiate the claim. Ms Marchant could provide no proof that she was refused promotion or transfer as she had not even applied for it. If the company had had a lawyer present, she could be made to look silly on this claim and this could harm the rest of her case. It is also important to go to the tribunal armed with all the relevant facts both to put your case, and to rebut employers' claims. Ms Marchant did not know about the men's training, though the employer did. Incidentally one of the five men was due to be witness for Ms Marchant and would have thus been able to describe his training and his actual work. But the union representative decided he was not necessary. The tribunal remarked on this and said he would have been useful.

Hobson v. Rowntree Mackintosh Ltd.

Mrs Hobson operates a machine which puts cellophane wrappers on boxes of Black Magic chocolates. She claimed equal pay with men working machines which wrapped Kit Kats. The company asserted that the men were 'concerned with the product which is to be consumed by the customer, whereas the applicant is concerned only with the outer wrapping'. The tribunal (on a majority decision only) decided to accept this and ruled that because the men were handling unwrapped chocolate bars, as opposed to the women handling boxes of ready wrapped chocolates, the men's 'responsibility to their employers with regard to the product, which goes out to the customer, is therefore of a different nature from that of the applicant'. The extent of Rowntree's genuine commitment to equal pay, incidentally, was exposed by evidence concerning the way the wage structure was changed at the end of 1975 to 'comply' with the Equal Pay Act. Whereas before there had been 'male piece work' and 'female piece work' grades, these were now combined into 'general piece work'. The men in 'general piece work', however, were able to preserve their advantage in pay terms by the subtle distinction of being labelled 'Piece work A'.

Some general points

The terms *of practical importance* and a *material difference* need to be distinguished from each other. The paragraph of the Act which deals with like work says any differences in two jobs must not be of *practical importance*. A *material difference* can be proved as a separate option after this; even if two jobs are established as like work or equivalent (job evaluated) work a material difference other than sex could still abolish the claim. It is difficult to separate these two ideas in practice however, and there is a tendency to use the two synonymously. Ms Marchant's job above, did not (like the men's) involve doing minor repairs or five weeks training and these differences were found to be of practical importance. However, despite like work being established above, the women could not claim equal pay because of the material difference of "responsibility" or "extra obligations" of the men.

This can lead to seeming contradictions. Many tribunal decisions state that what actually happens in the job is important for comparison and not the job description or job title, and then go on to find some material difference, even after establishing that the actual work done is similar.

Other points also arise from the tribunal decisions so far. Tribunals do not help where there are no men's jobs to compare women's with (see case 5). They can only establish equality claims and cannot help where a woman feels she is not paid *enough* (as Ms Hofmann case 4). They tend to support job evaluation or grading exercises, if agreed by management and union, even if the women feel they have been graded wrongly all along.

All in all, first conclusions indicate that equal pay problems are better sorted out in the workplace, and a tribunal used only as a last resort.

THE STRUCTURE OF TRIBUNALS

Industrial tribunals are a relatively new development. They are part of the *civil law* system of the country. Civil law is concerned with disputes between individuals. A person bringing a civil action has to establish that he has suffered some 'wrong' or denial of his rights for which he is entitled to 'damages' or compensation. Companies and other institutions are given a legal personality to enable them to sue and be sued in the same way as individuals.

Normally civil actions are pursued through the high court or the county court. Industrial tribunals were established to provide a more informal way of dealing with cases arising from recent labour law. Here is how the various aspects of *civil* law enforcement relate:

You will see that tribunals have *lay* members with practical experience of industrial affairs on the management and the union side. The idea was that cases could be resolved by applying practical common sense rather than rigid legal procedures. The role of the chairperson would be to advise on interpretation of the law and legal procedure.

The intention was that tribunals should be so informal that employees presenting their own cases would be at no disadvantage. But in practice tribunals have moved more towards legal formality, which weighs against the unrepresented employee.

Legal formality is bound to increase as legal precedents are established and case law is built up. Decisions made by ordinary tribunals do not set 'precedents' for other tribunals to follow. But decisions by the Employment Appeals Tribunal and the Appeal Courts do. So as more and more cases go to the EAT, case law builds up. And this case law is then quoted in future tribunal cases. Consequently the lay person is at a greater and greater disadvantage.

The exercise that follows is based on actual tribunal cases and will help you both to see how the law has operated in practice, and to think about how similar cases could be handled through negotiations.

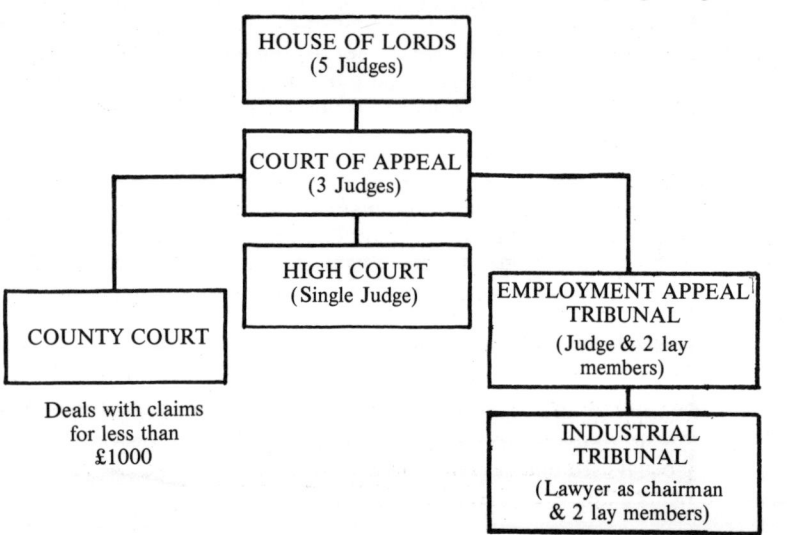

Case A

Ms V. I. Pitman brought a case against her employers at a Birmingham tribunal. The basis of Ms Pittman's claim was that she was underpaid in her job as a site clerk. Ms Pittman was the only clerical worker employed by the company, Stephell Ltd, on that particular site. The female clerical workers employed by the company on its other sites were all part-time.

Case B

Ms P. M. Iliffe claimed at a Leicester tribunal that she was doing the same work as a male employee of the company, GDS Transport Ltd, but getting £4 a week less. In other words the woman was doing like work to the man. But the kind of work the man was employed to do involved more responsibility, and his pay was set higher to reflect that expectation. In fact, the man "consistently failed to undertake" the more responsible work which might have justified higher pay, with the result that his job was in practice the same as Ms Iliffe's.

What the tribunals said

Case A

The decision went against her because the tribunal was unable to find any other job it was prepared to compare with hers. The tribunal decided that none of the male workers on the site was doing the same or broadly similar work to Ms Pittman. Having found no comparable jobs the tribunal dismissed the application. (COIT 432/180)

This decision is an ominous one for women in low-paid "women only" jobs. Instead of assessing what a man would have been paid to do Ms Pittman's job, and raising her pay to that level, the tribunal could only satisfy itself there was no one doing an identical job in the company and throw out her claim. Future revisions in equal pay legislation must take account of this problem. Low pay relative to men's is not just the problem of women working alongside men – it is also a feature of the many jobs where employers hire only women. The law at present allows tribunals to discriminate against the latter, much larger, group.

Case B

Having studied the two jobs, the tribunal announced it "...is not satisfied that the work which he does is substantially different from that which is performed by the applicant – not so different as to justify it being described as something which is not broadly similar."

Despite this Ms Iliffe *lost* her case. She lost it because the kind of work the man was employed to do would have involved more responsibility, and his pay was set higher to reflect that expectation. In fact, as the tribunal admitted, the man "consistently failed to undertake" the more responsible work which might have justified higher pay, with the result that his job was in practice the same as Ms Iliffe's. But the tribunal only has to show that the pay anomaly was due to a material difference (other than the sex difference) between her case and his. And the original *mistaken* assessment of the man's ability, the tribunal decided, *was* such a difference. (COIT 486/216)

Ludicrous decisions, like this, do not increase workers' faith in industrial tribunals. Having decided that the two jobs in question were the same in *practice*, the tribunal should have awarded equal pay. This decision can only encourage companies to specify more responsibility in the jobs men are taken on for, even if the actual work never matches up to the specifications.

Labour Research Department 1976

Role play

Study the make-up of tribunals. Enact a hearing. Discuss Cases A and B.
Have a panel of three, with at least one woman. Brief the student making the claim and the one as the employer.
A reading of 'Equal pay and the law' should furnish the necessary legal criteria for dealing with various types of claim.

Topic 3   Mixing it!

The tensions and stresses between the sexes; social concepts of 'natural' and 'cultural' and the different standards applied to social behaviour.

Aims

(1) To distinguish between patterns of behaviour and activity.
(2) To demonstrate comprehension of material presented by extracting relevant information.
(3) To recognise bias in selective presentation of information.
(4) To propose reasoned solutions to problems and assess alternative solutions.

Initial exercise

Write down three or four definitions of each of these terms: slut and slag.

Discuss

(1) Which sex are they usually addressed to?
(2) Are they complimentary?
(3) Do your definitions include, or could they include any men?
(4) What are the equivalent terms used for men? Are they complimentary?
(5) Are these examples of male chauvinism in language?
(6) Define male chauvinism.

Lyn Owen investigates the case of a girl on a building site who hauled the Guvnor before a tribunal

When the girl labourer swore—and got the sack

ON ONE SIDE of the grey municipal room, ranged on uncomfortable chairs, sat a cluster of very middle-class looking, spit-and-polish black gentlemen, confident and meekly decent. On the other, a bunch of strained, unhealthily frail, unkempt girls In the middle, bewildered behind their bench, sit a businessman, a lawyer, and a housewifely looking person, who is in fact a well-known unionist. This is an industrial tribunal and nothing is what it seems.

The chief black gent is far from middle class. He has struggled up via long skilled labour from sweeping snow in the Tottenham Court Road. Now an entrepreneur, his own counsel has suggested he's regarded as an unsatisfactory employer; he himself admits there have been complaints that he has left wage packets short. His second-in-command blithely admits to swearing, and being sworn at by workers. Two of the girls were his workers. But they too are not what they seem. Though they are the new London poor and look it, they're not ghosts of the sweatshops, but ex-academic middle class, far from frail, they're building labourers, accepted as quick and reliable workers, amazing at bashing down walls.

Immediately the boss's pay record and the swearing seem less outrageous. What is more, the question in dispute is not that the boss has oppressed the girls, but that they've oppressed him — one of them, that is Janet Krangel, a 23-year-old from Barnsbury. She has ferociously attacked him, verbally. And true to his great original Mr Gladstone Taylor, the boss, finds his puritan conscience shocked, and sacked her.

Janet sees it differently. She alleges discrimination. Several men swore violently at Taylor, her counsel alleges, and survived. The other side says not — everyone furiously abused each other on site, those in charge included, especially on pay day. But not the Guvnor. Though he wasn't usually there then.

Weeks are spent assessing what happened. The tribunal emerges divided. The majority, two men, say no discrimination. The woman unionist, yes.

The male tribunal members showed incredulity that Janet Krangel could have genuinely wanted to be a building worker for life. Surveying the motley ladies with their air of squats and communes, they questioned whether her repeated visits to labour exchanges asking for building work wasn't a ploy to keep her comfortably unemployed. Had she thought of entering building as a typist?

No compromiser, no leadslinger

But Janet Krangel, though no compromiser, was no social security leadswinger. She is part of a deliberate young women's movement into wider job spheres — and even more part of graduate unemployment, which has made plumbers of physical education instructors, gardeners of industrial psychologists, carpenters of liberal arts men. She has spent a year working in building cooperatives, made up partly of graduate architects who in the current slump are unable to get work. A group of her women friends, some ex-architects, have got craft training, and are working away as carpenters, plumbers, plasterers, painters, and car mechanics at sites all over London.

Janet has two applications, two years running, to the Construction Industry's Training Board behind her, for a bricklaying apprenticeship, six months hunting round 28 sites, numerous head offices, direct labour outfits, letters to all big firms, and eventually, help from doubtful Job Centres after application to MPs. All, until this job, fruitless.

Most women, she affirms, are poorly paid (currently an average £40 to the male £70 because they are channelled into special women's jobs, and about 90 per cent — as opposed to 10 per cent of men — are unskilled. Gradually a group of likeminded girls have gathered, so they now call themselves Women in Construction.

Some, along with young, ex-academic craftsmen, live in one of the many empty houses in a derelict inner London area bought up by speculators for young professionals no longer able to afford to "gentrify" them, now rebought by the council, no longer able to save them precisely because of bulk administrative spending and lack of actual building skills.

Whole streetsful of such houses have become the bare temporary ramshackle dwellings of West Indians, teachers, students, lecturers, doctors, nurses, social workers, PhDs. But the trail the women follow is tough. The Sex Discrimination Act has made the task more possible, but still a battle.

Just hunting for jobs fostered their aggression. At job centres they told Janet, "it's an odd thing for a woman to do — don't blame me if they fob you off with excuses." At sites, "They were overt before the Act, but now they're very subtle. At least then you could argue, now they just blank off with a whole lot of excuses."

There was only an opening at all, she suspects, because the rates were very low, "£45 for a 47½ hour week." Only at the bottom of the industry can women creep in. "And the foreman said, 'I don't know how long you'll last.'"

The men were bemused and shocked until I explained what I was doing, and showed them I worked hard. You had to prove yourself, and fight to get the hard jobs. I trained myself to lift cement bags — hard to do from scratch — and get used to the scaffolding. I shifted hardcore and timber." A worker told the tribunal he was amazed by her proficiency at knocking down walls; the boss said he was satisfied.

Another of the girls joined her to do plasterers' labouring and joint laying, and concreting, the heaviest jobs on site. "The problem then was being criticised by the others for working too fast. You had to explain, then they'd understand. After a bit I learned to skive, so as not to become unpopular. It's a real art. Much more exhausting than working."

Much was made in Janet's dismissal case of "a poor attendance record." Her employer first submitted he'd sacked her for poor time keeping, and sent a solicitor's statement saying she worked only three out of five days a week. Faced with documentary evidence to the contrary he had to withdraw it. He admitted to the court the average hours of his regular men were 36 out of a possible 47½. When shown that Janet's record was better, he said "I'm sorry. I should have said the average hours were 45."

While other girls on better sites found the men eventually accepted them and forgot the difference, on Janet's site it got worse; just as general resentment of married women working has worsened as jobs shrink, even in professions like teaching.

She felt threatened with the sack when — wanting a couple of days break — she asked for money owing, holiday pay, and "the week-in-hand." a week's arrears of wages withheld throughout the industry until departure. No one had explained the week-in-hand everywhere went with leaving, and when the boss said "Oh, you want to be paid up do you? You cannot have your week unless you terminate employment," she thought it was a hint of the boot.

She effed and blinded

The following week, no sub, which the boss said he offered her, holiday pay, or week-in-hand appeared in her pay packet. Like many of the workers on payday, with £31 to take home, she effed and blinded. Unlike them, she took it up with the boss. It was then the row occurred which sent her packing. Janet says she swore after getting the sack, the boss says she swore before, and that no one before had ever told him — as opposed to the foreman or ganger — "You effing bastard, you don't care."

There is, however some justice in the argument of the employer's counsel: that if the boss was an unsatisfactory employer, he was so to both sexes equally. So much of the treatment which led to Janet's arguing violently with the boss — and it is this which offended him, not the words used — he distinguished between "violent swearing, and the loose kind of swearing you hear everywhere in the street" is part of the industry in general. Men are hired and fired on whim, favour, and patronage, in many areas of the building industry, and often respond by turning up irregularly and working erratically in as cavalier way.

The worse the conditions are, the greater the technical sins they must commit, for which they can be arbitrarily rounded on. Who keeps exactly to a ten minute unpaid teabreak and a 30 minute unpaid lunch, when they have to walk half a mile to a loo, and take half an hour to wash their hands clean enough to eat, queuing for a hosepipe of soapless cold water?

Who doesn't pause for a smoke shovelling and heaving hundredweight cement bags and stirring it, with no mechanical aids?

The union feels that women entering the industry would help to change all this. "The union" says Janet "thinks women won't put up with such appalling conditions. They're not conditioned to unnecessary danger, for the sake of bravado. I think women would change conditions — just the way that men when they went into the catering trade wouldn't work the way the women there were conditioned to — non-stop, for next-to-nothing, the way they work at home. The men refused and conditions improved."

As to the basic (as opposed to unnecessary) filth and danger, and the heavy work, they were no worry for women. "Women are much tougher than people imagine. And if the construction industry isn't fit for women it isn't fit for human beings."

SOCIAL RELATIONS 49

Janet Krangel: a woman who talked back to the boss

Guardian 18 December 1978

Overheard

I was walkin' down this f.....' road the wind in my f.....' face, the rain squelchin' in my f.....' shoes and I thought 'F..... me, this can't get any worse' I got, in, banged the f.....' gate, kicked the bleedin' cat, knocked over a f.....' bottle of milk and made love to the wife.

Barman
'And what would the little woman like to drink, then? Babycham?'

'There was a lot of language going on in there.' (Attributed to Colin Addison, manager of Derby County about incidents in the dressing room at half time in the match against Arsenal which they were losing 2-0. In the second half, Derby scored three goals to win.)

Compare and discuss

(1) Is the *Mirror* article sympathetic?
(2) Is it 'natural' for men to swear? Define 'natural'.
(3) Why was it not expected that the woman labourer would swear?
(4) Was she sacked for swearing? If she did swear, what were the circumstances?
(5) Define 'cultural' (cf. 'natural/cultural').

Written exercises

(1) What is the difference between 'ungentlemanly' and 'unladylike'?
(2) How do we learn what role we play in society and how is it defined?

Philip lost his temper while he and the Queen were visiting Oman during their Middle East tour.

Pandemonium broke out in the small desert town of Nizwa.

Crowds moved in on the Queen completely cutting her off from her husband, who is renowned for his colourful language.

Safe

Then came an amazing sequence of events as Prince Philip – clearly worried about the Queen's safety—searched frantically for her.

With the temperature in the 90s, he was in shirt sleeves for the first time on the three-week tour which ends today.

He could not see the Queen and did not realise she was safe.

He kept asking newsmen: "Where is the Queen? Do you know? Where is the Queen?"

He managed at last to reach the Queen's original Cadillac and jumped in closing the door.

Then he realised there was no driver.

The Prince at first opened the door gently, then kicked it and stormed out saying: "It's bloody hot in there. It's like an oven. Where's my driver?"

He paused for a moment to wipe sweat from his forehead and said: "Bloody hell".

The Prince then spotted his own car about to drive past him. He banged on the roof and it stopped.

As he walked to it, another car driven by a soldier of ruler Sultan Qaboose's personal guard drew up with a piercing klaxon going full blast.

It was then that Prince Philip—putting his hands over his ears—bellowed at the driver: "Switch that bloody thing off, you silly f----." and thumped on the roof.

He got into his car and was driven off to find the Queen.

The rest of the party were still fighting to get to their cars.

Lady Susan Hussey, one of the Queen's ladies-in-waiting, spotted me and called: "I'll stick by you."

She grabbed my shirt and with another newsman bringing up the rear I shouldered a path through the crowd.

Prince Philip's language has landed him in the spotlight many times before. Samples include:

TO photographers in Scotland: "Did you get a picture of my left cart-hole?"

TO photographers in Jamaica: "You bloody load of clots."

DAILY Mirror

8p

Friday, March 2, 1979

BLOODY FURIOUS

Philip blows his top in the desert

PRINCE PHILIP lost his cool in the scorching desert sun yesterday. He rounded on a driver blazing away on his car horn and yelled: "Switch that bloody thing off, you silly f----."

Then he banged his fist down on the roof of the car.

PHILIP: Searched frantically

ALLOTT. We're not here to seek sexual stimulation, Catherine. We're here to peruse a beautiful and seemingly mysterious object, and to set it down — curiously — as objectively as we can.
BRENDA. It's alus a woman, sir.
SAUNDERS. Women have always been the subject of the very greatest art.
  (*Pause: they look at* SAUNDERS.)
  Because all the greatest artists, you see, have always been men.
GILLIAN. We know why, don't we, Sammy?
ALLOTT. I don't know why. Have you some information on the subject you've been keeping from us, Jilly?
GILLIAN. They like contemplating their human slaves.
WARREN. What slaves?
SAUNDERS. Who's a slave?
GILLIAN. Us. We're slaves.
MOONEY. Who keeps you in slavery?
GILLIAN. You do.
MOONEY. Me?
CATHERINE. *Men.*
WARREN. Bollocks.
GILLIAN. That's a man's answer to everything .... *Bollocks*.
MOONEY. I don't like women swearing... I've told you that before.
GILLIAN. Piss off!

ALLOTT. You could say that women have never had the *consciousness* to become artists — there are exceptions, but I mean as a general rule.

WARREN. Yeh, but, sir ...
SAUNDERS. I mean, don't you think that it would be extraordinary, Mr Allott, that something that has been denied women for so long should have taken all this time to emerge — I mean, their natural but frustrated capacity to be great thinkers, great composers, great artists, great poets ... great originators of thought and feeling? It seems humanly impossible that if this is an intrinsic part of the female temperament it should never have shown itself in any of these forms.
CATHERINE. Yeh... but that's the point, i'n it? In women it's been made *unnatural*.
WARREN. Piss off.
CATHERINE. You piss off!

BRENDA. Have we started?
CARTER. Not yet, my darling. (*Embraces her.*)
BRENDA. Get off... (*Stays in his embrace, however.*) That coffee does terrible things to your stomach.
MATHEWS. Come a bit closer and I might do something better.
BRENDA. Piss off. (*Sways with* CARTER *in embrace.*)
WARREN. I don't think women should swear, as a matter of fact.
MATHEWS. Neither do I.
BRENDA. Why not?
WARREN. I'll tell you why ... I've never heard *one* who can do it with conviction.
BRENDA. Fuck off.
WARREN (*to* CARTER). There's a first time, you see, for everything.

from *Life Class* by David Storey
Jonathan Cape, London, 1975

Additional Material   Natural/Cultural

It is also often said that men and women are born not just with biological differences, but with psychological ones too. Men are said to be naturally dominant, aggressive, and independent. Women are said to be naturally passive, meek, and dependent. Therefore, this view goes, men are naturally best fitted to deal with the harsh conditions outside the cosy domestic scene, while women are best fitted to stay within the domestic ambit. If women do take paid work, then it is best for them to stick to tasks such as teaching, nursing, cleaning, and so on, as these most closely reflect their biological role. This is what nature intended. Any other system would be unnatural.

The curious thing is, nature seems to have worked rather differently in other societies. Probably the most famous demonstration of this was made by the American anthropologist Margaret Mead. In her book *Sex and Temperament in Three Primitive Tribes* (1935) she describes three tribes in New Guinea. They each considered "natural" a system of sex-roles quite different, not only from our own, but also from the others.

In one tribe, the Arapesh, both sexes acted in a way our society thinks of as typically feminine. Both men and women were gentle and passive, and they shared equally the tasks of bringing up children.

In another tribe, the Mundugumor, both sexes acted in a way our society would consider typically masculine. Women as well as men were aggressive and independent, and both sexes detested the business of childbirth and child-rearing.

In the third tribe the situation was more like our own, in that men and woman played different roles: but the roles tended to be the reverse of those our society considers "natural." In this tribe, the Tchambuli, it was the women who were the practical, managing ones, and the men the ones who spent their time in gossip, shopping, and making themselves look attractive.

Other studies of other societies confirm Mead's basic point: the idea of what the "natural" sex-roles are can vary widely from one society to another. This casts doubt on the idea that our society—where men and women tend to live very different lives—is simply the result of nature wanting it that way.

Sociologists usually prefer another explanation. This is that people actually *learn* their sex-roles. As a male child grows graduates, men outnumber by six to one. As university academics, the proportion is more like ten to one—and among society. The same goes for female children, who have to learn what it is to be "feminine."

In other words, "male" is not the same as "masculine," nor "female" the same as "feminine." This is a crucial difference. Sociology draws a distinction between "sex" and "gender." "Sex" refers to the *biological* facts: most obviously, that females have one type of genitals, males another. "Gender," on the other hand, is a *cultural* term: it refers in this case to the ways a society expects the two sexes to behave. "Masculine" and "feminine" are descriptions of gender. "Male" and "female" are descriptions of sex.

It is widely held that the differences between the sexes are very great. But much recent research has underlined the similarities. Ann Oakley, in *Sex, Gender and Society* (1972) concludes that "most differences *between* the sexes ... are not as great as the individual differences *within* each sex." In other words, the differences between man and woman are sometimes less than the differences between man and man, or between woman and woman.

New Society 28 November 1978

A school recipe to 'turn the boys into pansies'

Express Staff Reporter

A SCHOOLBOY who is needled because he has to take needlework and cookery lessons has been ordered to get on with it —because of the Sex Discrimination Act.

Pint-size victory

By JAMES LEWIS

A LICENSING bench in Lancashire decided yesterday that a landlord's refusal to serve women with drinks in a pint glass was not sufficient reason to deprive him of his licence.

Mr John O'Rourke, landlord of the Swan and Railway Hotel, at Radcliffe, told the bench at Bury, that he would serve women with pints "if they conform with what I wish," but added that he had never been asked for a pint by any woman who had not been barred from his pub.

Miss Susan Ashby, a college lecturer, who objected to the renewal of the licence, said that when she asked Mr O'Rourke for a pint of shandy, he replied that he only served ladies with half pints. This, she contended, was an offence under the Sex Discrimination Act.

Mr O'Rourke said he had never even offered Miss Ashby even half a pint because she was barred from his house. Asked when the bar took effect he replied: "The moment you walked through the door."

Mr Janos Kowalczyk, a male nurse, said that when he asked for a pint of mild for his friend, Miss Jane McIver, Mr O'Rourke served two half pint glasses. "When I asked for a pint glass Mr O'Rourke poured the drink away and told us to get out."

Guardian 17 March 1978

At Cabinteely
we stop for the first pint
and a couple of rounds of the native culture.
Here, if you imbibe the culture
for long enough,
it's called nature.
(from: *Home: Going or coming*
    by Donal Carroll)

women's groups have concentrated on what they see as sexism in the media: on TV, in advertisements, and so on. Their criticism is that the dominant image of woman is either as a "sex-object" or as wife-and-mother, and that this acts as a form of hidden propaganda, helping to maintain the idea that women should only ever play a subordinate role.

'CHIVALRY INSULTS ME'

When I take a cigarette out of its pack, I resent a well-meaning male companion seizing the matchbox from my other hand and doing the chivalrous thing. I can also put on my coat with greater ease when left to find the armholes for myself. And I get a crick in the neck from swivelling it to accommodate gentlemanfolk who keep on switching to the outside of the pavement every time we cross roads together.

'You're being rather petty, aren't you?' sigh the men to whom I voice my objections. 'There are a lot of more important women's issues than *this*.' But, for me, that's no reason to suffer in silence the daily indignities of chivalry.

The compliments of courtesy are a bothersome bugbear. For, when I am in conversation with a male and he suddenly leaps forward to open a door for me, I am all too unpleasantly aware that he has momentarily ceased to regard me as an individual; instead I've become a representative of my sex for whom convention requires that the door be opened. It isn't even chivalry most of the time; it's just automatic behaviour. Yet I'm supposed to feel grateful for it.

Well, I don't appreciate anything that's executed purely for tradition. 'But it's *respect*,' they complain. I want to be respected for my abilities at my job, for my wit, compassion, sense of responsibility – if I have them – and not for the accident of my gender. For me, it's the motivation behind an action that makes it important. If a friend helps me move house, I'm genuinely grateful. If people remember my birthday, I'm truly touched. For it is me, as an individual, they have put themselves out for – and that's wonderful.

And it's an equally warm glow that I get from the unsolicited assistance of strangers. Yes, I'm very thankful if a man carries a suitcase that is manifestly too heavy for me, or opens the door when I'm loaded up with four bags of shopping. For that shows genuine awareness of another human being's predicament. It has nothing to do with maleness and femaleness – it's the giving of assistance where assistance is needed. Just as I think it my place to give up my seat on a train or a bus to a pregnant woman or an elderly man. But chivalry, that's something else.

One of the dictionary definitions of chivalry is 'inclination to defend the weaker party'. How did it ever get diluted down to the execution of insignificant actions that a weaker party can manage quite well for itself? I will not be otherwise convinced. Those gentlemanly actions that masquerade as 'common courtesies' are just subtle reinforcements of role distinction. The gentlemanly act reminds me that I am supposed, after all, to be a lady. The selective nature of chivalry bears that out. Ingratiating male companions with one eye on the bedroom door are more inclined to perform its pleasantries than the surly commuter varieties, who sit squarely in their seats and stare straight past the elderly woman strap-hanging in front of their noses. My mother tells me she fell over in the street when she was eight months pregnant. And, although she collapsed right by a bus stop, no one came to her aid for fear of losing their place in the queue.

The age of chivalry is starting to die but it's still by no means dead. Nor is its lifeblood only kept flickering by men who are old enough to have fought in World War II. Recently I came to a compromise with a lunch companion, who was still the right side of forty. When we got up to leave, I protested that I really did wish to put my coat on alone. 'Oh very well,' he capitulated. 'I'll go to the gents so you can slip it on while I'm away!'

But I've met him since and now he doesn't even bat an eyelid. That, from him, really *is* courtesy. *DENISE WINN*

Company June 1979

In 1877...
many trade unions did not allow women to join, and the Trades Union Congress (TUC) declared that a woman's place was in the home.

Even the history of trade unions usually comes across as the story of men. But women too played their part...

Trade unions were illegal in the early years of the 19th century, yet there are records of women taking militant action at work from as early as 1832, when 1,500 women who made the cards for weaving machines went on strike for equal pay. This was only 8 years after unions became legal again — the women had lost no time in organising.

But at the same time, newly-invented machinery had begun to threaten some craftsmen's jobs, so these men didn't want women joining the unions too — they had enough to do protecting themselves and *their* jobs. Industries with a long tradition of female labour, like weaving in the Lancashire cotton mills, had mixed unions. But on the whole, women workers were forced to organise themselves separately.

It was the 'Match Girls' — 1,400 brave women who worked at the Bryant & May match factory in London's East End — who changed the course of trade union history when they came out on strike in 1889. Their pay was so bad and their working conditions so unhealthy, that a group of socialists and feminists boycotted Bryant & May products and published articles about the conditions in the factory. The managers retaliated by sacking one of the women workers — and the rest walked out immediately, in protest.

The example of the strength and unity of the 'Match Girls' impressed the rest of the male-dominated trade union movement, who soon began to accept women into their unions as equals.

Left: Emma Paterson, who in 1874 began organising women workers into the Women's Protective & Provident League. In 1875, she put the first equal pay proposal to the TUC. This policy was finally agreed in 1888.
Right: Mary Macarthur, who began the National Federation of Women Workers in 1906. The work of these 2 women helped to bring nearly half a million working women into unions by 1914, when the First World War broke out. By the end of the Second World War, there were 2 million women members.

Virago Ltd

100 years later...

Topic 4 Something larger than me

Aim

To distinguish between others in the sense of individuals and 'society' as a collective.

Read and discuss

(1) Why are more women joining trade unions?
(2) Why is their membership not reflected in the unions' hierarchy?
(3) Do certain male attitudes make it more difficult for women to join unions?
(4) Why did some nineteenth-century unions refuse to allow women to join?
(5) What have things like childcare and abortions to do with trade unions?
(6) Why has the recent increase in unemployment affected women more than men?
(7) Do the jobs many women do discourage them from joining trade unions?
(8) Are women at your workplace encouraged to join?
(9) Do women have the same choices men have – career, promotion etc., at your workplace.
(10) Do unions exist in your firm? Are you encouraged to join?

For every one woman official

there are...

● ● ● ● ● ● ● ● ● ●
● ● ● ● ● ● ● ● ● ●
● ● ● ● ● ● ● ● ● ●
● ●

...32 men.

Even the unions with a mainly female membership – such as nurses, cleaners, shop workers – hardly ever send a woman to represent them at the TUC.

Written exercises

(1) Are the interests of women trade unionists any different from those of men?
(2) Do unions remain predominantly masculine though women are the fastest growing section? What can be done to change this?
(3) Are women who want to work 'penalised' for having children? (cf. cartoon)

Research (or longer written work)

(1) Find out if there is a 'hidden history' of women workers in your locality. (Local library, newspapers, trades council may help.)
(2) Write a letter inviting a local man and woman trade unionist to speak to your group explaining why you are inviting both.
(3) Write a discussion paper explaining the advantages and disadvantages of joining a trade union. (Some extra reading may be required.)
(4) Compare maternity leave (and assorted benefits, including retention of seniority at work on return after pregnancy) in this country with other EEC countries.

It just doesn't figure...

There are over half a million members in the local government workers' union **NALGO**. Nearly half of them are women. 95 per cent of branch chairmen are in fact **MEN**, 84 per cent of branch secretaries are **MEN**

These figures showing the number of women in trade unions and the number of women occupying positions of influence was produced over a year ago
These figures showing the number of women in trade unions and the number of women occupying positions of influence were produced over a year ago by the Equal Pay and Opportunities Campaign.

Recent figures, as far as can be obtained, show that the proportion of women in the union hierarchy is falling.

UNION	Membership m	f	Percentage of women members	National Executive m	f	Full-time officials m	f	TUC delegates m	f
APEX	62,438	75,278	55%	11	4	5	1	10	3
ASTMS	351,000	62,000	18%	23	1	65	5	19	1
AUEW eng. Sec.	1,038,720	166,000	14%	9	.	186	1	35	.
Bakers	30,122	20,325	40%	14	4	25	1	10	.
COHSE	42,420	101,059	70%	27	1	35	5	8	.
CPSA	69,451	145,693	68%	18	8	24	4	22	8
CSU	29,108	17,676	38%	21	2	10	1	8	2
EETPU	361,193	52,996	13%	14	.	150	.	13	1
FTAT	73,857	10,243	12%	24	.	40	.	11	1
GMWU	592,073	290,283	33%	30	.	272	10	64	4
IRSF	23,093	31,827	58%	25	3	6	1	9	.
NALGO	357,942	267,221	43%	61	5	174	17	69	5
NUBE	58,118	48,957	46%	21	3	28	3	13	.
NUFLAT	32,187	30,268	48%	15	1	46	2	13	.
NUHKW	19,887	52,836	73%	23	2	29	2	11	1
NUPE	201,847	382,638	65%	20	6	120	2	29	4
NUT	66,896	197,453	75%	41	7	24	2	30	1
NUTGW	13,359	96,070	88%	10	5	34	6	11	5
SCS	85,000	17,000	17%	22	4	17	3	17	.
SOGAT	123,876	69,928	36%	30	2	67	3	31	5
TASS	128,895	15,571	11%	26	1	36	2	14	4
TGWU	1,511,000	289,000	16%	39	.	480	3	76	2
TSSA	55,600	15,705	22%	28	2	50	10	13	2
UPW	147,679	42,321	22%	14	5	11	1	12	2
USDAW	153,653	223,649	59%	16	1	129	4	21	5

UNION SPY

DURING the Trico womens' strike for equal pay two years ago, the Amalgamated Union of Engineering Workers sent out a letter appealing for support for the women members.

It began 'Dear Sir and Brother'. At that time the union had 62,000 women members. Nonetheless the message of the womens movement has been percolating through into the upper echelons of the AUEW.

This year the union's executive (all male) has voted to dispense with the 'Dear Sir and Brother' opening for all official correspondence.

In its place they are introducing the non-sexist term 'Dear Colleague'. The moderates who now control the union remain adamantly opposed to using 'Dear Brother/Sister.'

It smacks of extremism, apparently.

The 1970s have seen the most rapid growth of trade union membership in history, by three and a quarter millions to 12,128,000.
"We are told that we are unpopular, but we are not unpopular with working people," said Mr Murray. A significant factor in the growth has been the increasing number of women joining unions. In the last 10 years the total has jumped by 1.6 millions, an increase of more than 100 per cent.

Guardian September 1979

The married woman's role, as it has been pared down in modern times, is less than satisfying to the complete human being. Were childrearing, together with social welfare and a host of other tasks performed from the home, as in the 19th century, it might be a different matter. But it must be faced that, once the children are at school, the main occupation of a married woman is wielding a duster, an iron and a frying pan. The bulk of housework, say the industrial experts, demands the intelligence of a child of eight.

The unemployment rate for women, for example, increased by 53 per cent between 1976 and 1978, as compared with 9 per cent for men—although, during this period masses more women were being taken on, as well as being sacked, from work. Her figures, coupled with Rachel Nelson's, suggest such boundless mountain-ranges, of prejudice that women can be forgiven for feeling like giving up.

Observer September 1979

12 TUC aims

UNIONS WANT Complete equality of job opportunity for women with men.
Apprenticeships for girls on the same terms as they are available to boys.
Day release for further education for all young workers – girls as well as boys.
UNIONS WANT Complete equality of opportunity for girls with boys right through the educational system.
UNIONS WANT Women to have equal promotion opportunities with men.
UNIONS WANT Sick pay and occupational pension schemes for everybody at work – and everybody means women as well as men.
UNIONS SAY A woman should be entitled to paid maternity leave and to reinstatement in her previous job (or one of comparable status and grade) if she returns within nine months.
UNIONS CALL FOR The proper rate for the job for all workers, male and female, and an end to all pay discriminations against women workers.
UNIONS WANT Advice centres in local employment offices to assist women to return to paid employment after some years away from work.
Retraining and refresher courses for all women who wish to return to the same kind of job which they did before they had their children.
Training for all women who want to learn new skills and enter new fields of employment.
UNIONS OPPOSE Any moves to allow women to work on jobs or with materials which might endanger their health or of an unborn baby.
UNIONS SAY Employers must accept the need for women to work the hours which will enable them to meet their commitments as mothers or to assist them to care for their elderly dependants.
UNIONS SAY Local authorities should be obliged to provide day nurseries open throughout the day to assist working mothers and nursery school education should be available for children below school age.
Local authorities should also provide interesting activities for school children during holidays.
UNIONS SAY There must be no discrimination against any woman worker on grounds of her marital status.
UNIONS SAY Women are equal members of the community with men and all discriminations against them must be abolished.

How many of the jobs would you like to be considered for?

Virago Ltd

GREAT EXPECTATIONS

I WANT A WIFE...
to have dinner on the table when I get home;
to bear my children, to see they're properly dressed, fed and kept clean;
to entertain my friends;
to listen to my problems and to understand me and never to complain about what she has to put up with;
who won't interfere with my freedom especially when I want a night out with the boys;
who can manage on what she's given in the way of housekeeping money;
who never says: 'No, I'm too tired!'
to keep my house looking decent;

I WANT A HUSBAND...
to be the breadwinner;
go give me children and provide for them;
to take me out now and then; and to talk to occasionally, for a bit of company;
who comes home when he's expected and doesn't stay out all night;
who understands how much food costs nowadays;
who doesn't make too many demands;
who appreciates the effort I make keeping the house decent;

COUNTRY	LEAVE	PAY
Belgium	14 weeks @	60 per cent
France	14 weeks @	full pay + 1 year unpaid
Germany	14 weeks @	net wage + 18 for twins/premature
Italy	12 weeks @	80 per cent + 6 months at 30 per cent
Luxemburg	12 weeks @	50-75 per cent
Holland	12 weeks @	full pay

Predictably, these Bunny Girls got massive publicity for their message. And, sadly, they got their way. But many others are fighting to regain their dignity. Mayfair's Playboy Club had to close when 700 bunnies, croupiers and caterers voted on whether to join the Transport and General Workers Union. Their action was sparked off by the sacking of ten staff.

Read and discuss

(1) What qualifications are required for 'bunny girls'?
(2) What training is given?
(3) Estimate the duration of the job.
(4) What security is given?
(5) Is the title of the job patronising?
(6) Is there any consistency between the type of dress worn and the message?

Written exercises

(1) Make an application to the Playboy Club for a 'bunny job' whether you are male or female.
(2) Speculate on why she does not want to join.
(3) Write a job description for a 'bunny girl' (a) literally, (b) metaphorically.
(4) Write a letter to the bunny club (a) supporting the girl, (b) stating why you think this type of job emphatically requires a union.

Topic 5   Power relations between the sexes

Aims

(1) To evaluate and analyse information from a variety of sources.
(2) To determine the implications of a communication.
(3) To distinguish between subjective and objective knowledge.
(4) To select appropriate solutions and justify them.

Read and discuss

(1) How exceptional is French's view of the average marriage?
(2) Can marriage reduce women to a trivial fraction of their worth?
(3) Is the tone one of hostility or analysis or what?

The opposite Sex/the opposing sex?

So much for the natural relation between the sexes.
But you see, he doesn't have to beat her much, he surely doesn't have to kill her: if he did, he'd lose his maidservant. The pounds and pence by themselves are a great weapon. They matter to men, of course, but they matter more to women, although their labor is generally unpaid. Because women, even unmarried ones, are required to do the same kind of labor regardless of their training or inclinations, and they can't get away from it without those glittering pounds and pence. Years spent scraping shit out of diapers with a kitchen knife, finding places where string beans are two cents less a pound, learning to wake at the sound of a cough, spending one's intelligence in figuring the most efficient, least time-consuming way to iron men's white shirts or to wash and wax the kitchen floor or take care of the house and kids and work at the same time and save money, hiding it from the boozer so the kid can go to college – these not only take energy and courage and mind, but they may constitute the very essence of a life.

from *The Women's Room* by
Marilyn French, Sphere Books 1978

Overheard

50-year-old catering student, a mother of four, having worked all her life: 'I don't understand Women's Lib; I seem to have missed out on all the ecstasy.' (1972)

'I was just doing my job'.
(ex-wife of 'Buzz' Aldrin, first man on the moon)

'Everything a woman could give is *expected* of her as a wife. What's left?'
(battered wife from Newcastle 1979)

films exemplify the emphasis in many of the recent spate of films of extreme violence upon sexual assault and the degradation of women. The BBFC was stirred to note in its March 1976 Monthly Report that *Violated Angels* was only one of seven films that month to include rape—'a subject for which there seems to be a growing fashion in many parts of the world.' Chris Pettit shrewdly pointed out in *Time Out* that following the Second World War there was a kind of parallel: 'The Hollywood woman-in-jeopardy cycle reached a peak ... The overseas forces returned home to discover that during their absence women, by necessity, had achieved greater social, economic and sexual freedom. The immediate need was to rehabilitate women back into the home. Hollywood's post-war cultural propaganda was therefore predictably misogynist. Movie heroines, when not subjected to actual physical handicaps, were under psychological pressure. The message was plain, as Marjorie Rosen has noted in *Popcorn Venus*: "Men were arbiters of women's sanity—or insanity".' Perhaps the insistent submission of women in films of the 70s to humiliation, degradation and sexual violence is the price that is being vicariously exacted for the liberation movement.

This certainly seems to be the specific message of *Death Weekend*. In the opening scenes the heroine is shown asserting her domination over the weak and sexually maladjusted male (a voyeur who takes women to his home and then photographs them through one-way mirrors). Symbolically, she takes the wheel of his powerful sports car and shows herself the more reckless driver. It is while showing off her prowess that she arouses the fury of four moronic thugs, by driving them off the road. They demand revenge. Entering the man's house, they smash up his most treasured possessions, vomit over the furniture and finally kill him. Then the promise of the disreputable but apparently effectively inviting advertising campaign is fulfilled: 'They were going to rape her . . . one by one.' She was going to kill them . . . one by one.' In case the male chauvinist point is not entirely apparent, at the end of the film, after the girl has devised terrible deaths for her four tormentors, in a quick series of flashback shots the leader of the gang—the only good-looking and bright member of the group—suddenly appears to her eyes as sexually desirable. She is, in other words, clearly shown to have *desired* the rape which she has herself frustrated.

(4) Has the view of the catering student anything to do with the way in which Women's Lib (The Women's Movement) has been described in the popular press?
(5) In the piece on film, who has made the films involved?
(6) Is there evidence of men 'getting their own back'? How? Why?
(7) Are the two comments on marriage said in sadness or as a new beginning?

Written work

(1) Why is there a separate *Women's* Movement?
    How differently do women experience society from men?
    Who governs society and makes the rules?
(2) What changes have occurred since the origins of the Women's Movement?

Information Retrieval

Locate the figures for divorce and marriage over the past 5 years. Analyse and speculate on the results.

Double standard

What exactly is this double standard?
How do you learn it?
How does it affect you?

The double standard is the idea that, just as men and women behave differently in general, so it's natural and right that they behave differently when it comes to sex. Because the biology of the two sexes is not the same, people assume that their experience of sex, their needs for it and their attitudes towards it will also be different. So what's done by one is often discouraged in the other. As you grow older, you act out this idea more and more.

'You should not for a moment think that girls have no sexual physical sensations at all. These sensations are different from yours [boys], in that they tend to be rather vaguely spread throughout the body and seem to most girls just like general yearning sort of feelings – rather like looking at a beautiful sunset and wanting to keep it but not knowing how.'
PAULINE PERRY, *Your Guide to the Opposite Sex*, Pitman, 1970

Sex education – the only lesson for which we never had a practical

A lot of books have been written to explain sex to young people. These books soon make it clear that sex is one thing for boys and another for girls. Even the titles of some of the books tell you this: *Sex for Boys; Girls and Sex; Your guide to the Opposite Sex*. And the content (our italics):

Why do you think women are supposed to like men who treat them badly?
Do you ever hear women saying they like men who can dominate them?
What personal qualities do women find most attractive in men?
Are men attracted to women for the same reasons?

Double standard

Read and discuss

(1) Does it exist?
(2) Who generally defines the rules?
(3) Have you ever thought in these terms?
(4) Who is most likely to get hurt in a one-night stand? Why?
(5) What does the term 'promiscuity' mean to you?
(6) Under what circumstances are the four terms mentioned used?
(7) Do they imply something different than they actually mean?

The double standard means that boys and girls have to give different reasons to explain why they want sex.

Which person is most likely to get hurt in a one-night stand? Why?
Promiscuity is a word often used with disapproval. What does it mean to you?

I daren't tell him
My boyfriend and I are getting engaged but he doesn't know I'm not a virgin. I slept regularly with my last boyfriend and at the time I didn't think there was anything wrong with doing that, as I loved him and we were going to get married. However, things didn't work out and we broke up. Then I met Jim, my present boyfriend, and I love him so much that I feel we could wait till we get married before we have any sexual relations. Now I feel so cheap and dirty and ashamed of my previous relationship. I wish I was still a virgin. My problem is, Jim thinks I am a virgin and much as I would like to, I can't tell him.
    JOY, Scotland [a typical letter from a women's magazine]

All Virago Ltd, *The Gender Trap* Vol 2

GENERAL AND COMMUNICATIONS STUDIES

> People say things like:
> Men are like animals.
> Women don't like sex.
> All men are sex-mad.
> What's the matter with you – are you frigid?
>
> This makes it sound as though sexually man and woman have very little in common.

Rape 'Asking for it'

Read and discuss

(1) Are all rapes reported to the police? If not, why?
(2) Has the law on rape been changed recently? In what way?
(3) Has it been changed by a man or a woman?
(4) Are rape sentences adequate deterrents?
(5) How much does the 'double standard' play in rape?
(6) Do certain images of women in advertisements etc., contribute (however indirectly) to rape?
(7) Study the two pictures: what meanings are conveyed by the images?

Written work

(1) 'We live in a violent society of which rape is just a part': analyse and discuss.
(2) Is having a law on rape enough?
(3) Has the attitude to rape anything to do with the attitude to women in general?

Research

Collect details of how rape is dealt with in your local press. Is it presented from a point of myth or fact?

If you are a woman, you are –

A lady	OR	A tramp
A virgin	OR	A whore
A good girl	OR	A bad girl
To bring home to Mum	OR	To laugh about with the boys
To wed	OR	To bed
You do	OR	You don't
They love you	OR	They leave you
For keeps	OR	A bit on the side

Being weighed up on:

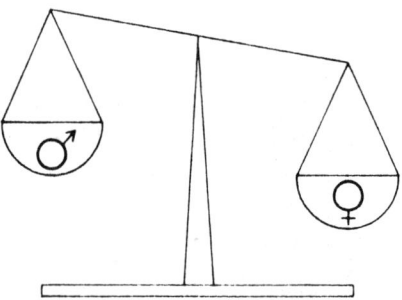

THE SCALES OF INJUSTICE

You've probably read about many rape cases in the newspapers, and the stories are often like this:
– A man was denied sex by his 'frigid' wife, so he went off and raped a young girl.
– A young man was accused of raping a girl outside a dance hall, but was let off because the court believed she actually led him to do it.
– A woman was raped in a dark street at night by a sexual maniac.

Such accounts, instead of trying to get to the truth, tend to support the popular myths about rape, which are that:

women deserve it;
women like it;
men are driven to it.

In a court case, which may take place if the man is identified, the woman has to disclose every detail of her personal life – whether she was a virgin, how many abortions she has had, etc. She has to 'prove' that she has been raped. If she is unmarried and not a virgin, that will be held against her. The attitude is that, if she has already had sex with several men, she may be likely to lead any man on, so one more won't make much difference. Often there are no women on the jury, so, having committed no crime, she is judged from the male point of view. Women's evidence is often thought of as unreliable, and likely to be a 'fantasy' to get their own back on husbands and boyfriends.

The whole emphasis is to protect the man against false prosecution. The 1975 House of Lords ruling makes it harder to convict the man – because he might have thought the woman willing even though she screamed and fought him.

Underlying this is the belief that women actually enjoy being raped; that they find violence sexually exciting, and that struggling and resisting are only a pretence. It's often said that there's 'no such thing as rape'. Try asking someone who's been raped.

The treatment of rapists is by no means harsh when compared with that for crimes such as theft and robbery. A very low proportion of those caught and arrested is actually convicted. In America, where rape is a much more serious problem than in this country, only 2% of rapes end in the cinviction of the rapist. Only 28% of rapes in the United States are thought to be reported (FBI figures) – a reflection of the social attitudes towards rape.

Disposal of adults convicted of full rape in 1973	
No. convicted	201
non-custodial sentences	
suspended sentence	7
other non-custodial	8
medical disposal	
hospital order	1
restriction order	3
custodial sentences	
detention centre	3
borstal training	16
under 2 years imprisonment	20
2-3 years	45
3-4 years	36
5 years and over	62
note: 'adult' means aged 17 and over	

64 GENERAL AND COMMUNICATIONS STUDIES

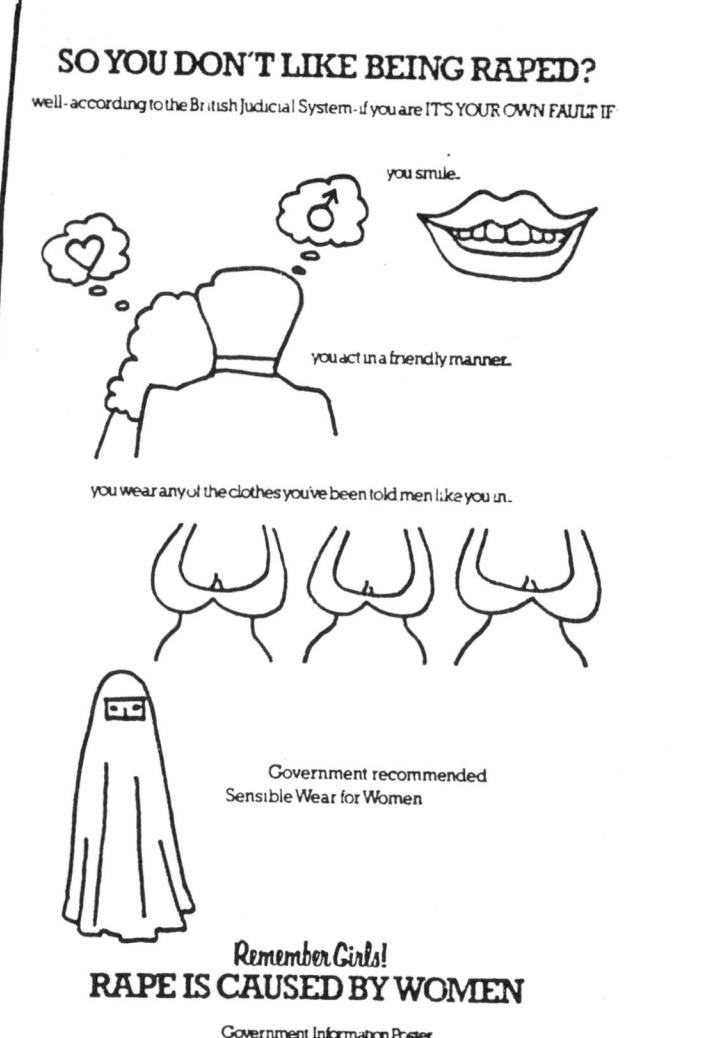

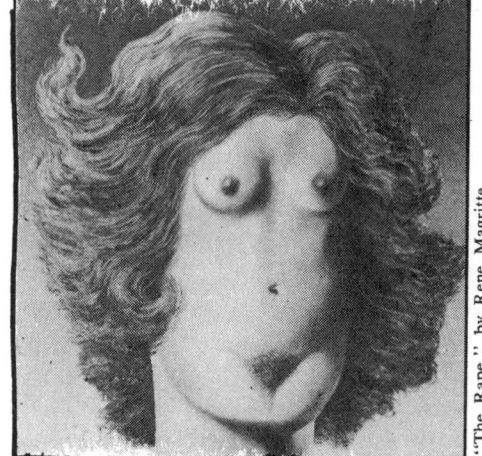

'Once in Cabinet we had to deal with the fact that there had been an outbreak of assaults on women at night. One minister suggested a curfew; women should stay at home after dark. I said, "But it's the men who are attacking the women. If there's to be a curfew let the men stay at home, not the women".'

— GOLDA MEIR

"The Rape," by Rene Magritte

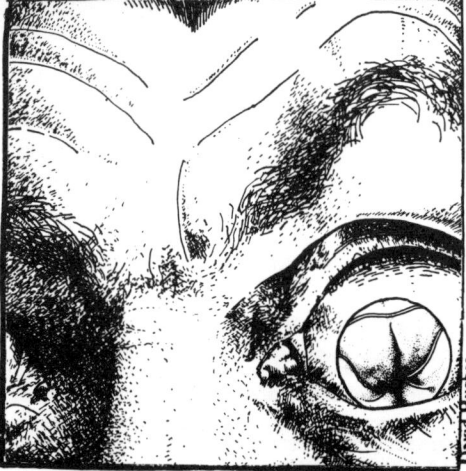

RAPE and FIGHTING BACK

WHAT IS RAPE?

MYTH: All women want to be raped.

FACT: Rape is not sexual intercourse at the wrong time, in the wrong place. It is an act of extreme violence against women. It can involve beating, choking, urinating or defecating on the woman. Knives, bottles and broomhandles have been used.

MYTH: Only bad women get raped.

FACT: In the experience of the Rape Crisis Centre, women of all ages, races and lifestyles have been raped.

MYTH: Rapists are sex-starved maniacs.

FACT: Men do not rape because of uncontrollable sexual urges. 63% of cases dealt with by the RCC in its first six months were planned. In 1975 in England and Wales, less than 2½% of convicted rapists were sent for psychiatric treatment.

MYTH: Rapists are always strangers in dark alleys.

FACT: Rape can happen in any place at any time. Rapists can be husbands, lovers, fathers, employers, the boy next door or the man who comes to read the meter.

The Rape Crisis Centre, PO Box 42, London N6 5BU.

Rape is a crime. The maximum sentence is life imprisonment, but it is very rare for this to be given. There is currently a proposal to reduce the maximum sentence to 7 years. The average sentence is about 4 years. But some people reckon that only half the rapes committed in Britain are reported to the police. If this is true, then hundreds of rapists are getting off scot-free.

The popular beliefs — or myths — about rape make it difficult for a woman to decide whether she should go to the police. She is often afraid they will not believe her. Or perhaps she just can't bear the thought of a medical examination by the police doctor, who is almost bound to be a man. *She* is the victim, but somehow she feels guilty herself. She knows very well that she didn't 'ask for it' or 'enjoy it', but these ideas are so deeply and widely accepted in our society that she often can't help questioning herself. One woman, a 49-year-old nurse, who was single and lived alone, was raped when a man broke into her flat at night. She said: 'I was too terrified and paralysed with fear to scream but did try to defend myself, without success ... (later) even with my family, there was a terrible feeling of shame and degradation, as though I myself had been guilty of a crime'.

Level 2

Subject Area: Mass Communications

The different methods of collecting, processing and packaging information with emphasis on the distinction between content and presentation.

Aims

(1) To extract and organise information from appropriate mass sources.
(2) To examine the availability of the concept of 'balance'.
(3) To distinguish between fact and opinion; news and comment.
(4) To recognise bias and selective presentation.
(5) To examine critically the role of the mass media.
(6) To use appropriate, acknowledged sources to present material, collated and processed, which demonstrates and defends a viewpoint.

Read and discuss

(1) Could the word 'censorship' be used here?
(2) Does the story offend anyone? Why?
(3) How does the editor know that people would not like to read 'that type of thing'? You are reading it.
(4) Who has the ultimate power over what goes into a newspaper?
(5) In '*overheard*' what standpoint are the stories presented from? Could they be presented from another point of view?
(6) Could the editor justify these on the basis of 'human interest'?
(7) Is either offensive? Why?

Initial written exercise

Have you ever read or seen on TV a report of an event you attended?
How did your experience compare with the report? (Did you have a different standpoint?)
Write a critical report of the last social event you attended (a) for the *Sun*, (b) for the *Guardian*, (c) for television news.
The limit is one page.
Compare and contrast. Analyse and speculate on any differences.

Not the sort of thing people want to read about at breakfast

A YEAR AGO I visited a hit man in one of Her Majesty's prisons. He told me that his mate's daughter was working in computers and earning £7,000 a year, and as I was earning less than half that at the Crucible, why was I still there?" I told him that it was exciting, exhilarating, demanding, involving, and good fun. "There must be something about it you don't like," he said. "Well," I explained, "it's a question of personalities. Occasionally somebody throws a tantrum, but that doesn't happen often. One of the worst things is dealing with bores when you're in a hurry; every time one particular bore comes into my office I think, 'Oh no, how am I going to get rid of him?'." The hit man leaned forward and said, "Just tell me his name."

He was joking, of course. But it was a comforting fantasy to fall back on when directors ranted on about poor houses or journalists threatened smear campaigns. Galloping paranoia is part of the every day life of your average press officer, like dead flies on the teeth of a happy motorcyclist. I often found that I was defending the press to the Crucible, and in the next breath defending the Crucible to the press. I belonged to the Crucible, but sometimes was seen to be a representative of the press — to such an extent that a director once shouted at me about a review just because I was nearer than the journalist who'd written it.

It's a pig-in-the-middle situation, which often becomes a defensive position, partly because publicity is such a nebulous subject. When crowds swarm in and a cast is playing to packed houses, they take the credit; but when tickets are being given away in their hundreds, the easiest thing to blame is a lack of publicity. I was once so desperate about a show that I dreamt an actor nagged me and I retaliated by saying we'd done all the usual things and we'd written 365 letters to head teachers and 294 to heads of English, and then I woke myself up by shouting, "Now what do you want me to do — streak down High Street?"

The Monty Python duo, Michael Palin and Terry Jones, were asked by a journalist if they were nervous about their play opening in the Studio. They told the journalist to imagine building a car from a DIY kit and then sitting in the passenger seat while someone else drove it in the Monte Carlo—and they'd not taken out insurance. A press officer can arrange interviews and persuade critics to review shows, but has no control over what's said or printed.

Some interviews never get printed at all. During the run of Romeo and Juliet, a journalist interviewed the stage manager about condoms being used as blood bags for every fight scene. Durex were filled with stage blood and strapped to the appropriate actors. That meant that the stage manager made frequent visits to the nearest Boots to stock up on Durex (he claimed that by the end of the run all the girls in Boots were leaping over the counter to serve him). The story was along the lines of The People's Right To Know: here is a little known fact, namely that 23 Durex were used in every performance of the Crucible's production of Romeo and Juliet — and twice that number on Thursdays and Saturdays. Alas, the piece was never printed. The journalist was told by his editor that it was "not the sort of thing people want to read about at breakfast."

One event that attracted a lot of publicity — but for which I take no credit whatsoever — was the time a dinosaur went missing. The stage manager rang the police who asked for a description. "It's nine feet tall," she said, "green, two front paws, two hind legs, a six-foot-long tail, and it's called Tyranosaurus Rex." "No distinguishing features, then," said the cop, and promised to keep an eye open.

Because the theatre is a service to the general public, Pete James has continually produced a very varied programme, and he also added a trendy shop and a hire department to the usual front-of-house catering facilities. Ratepayers have every opportunity to get their money's worth. A lady once told me enthusiastically that she and her husband went to the Crucible at least twice a month. I launched into what was supposed to be a discussion about the current production, but she interrupted: "Oh no, we don't go to see the plays — we go there to eat."

Guardian 18 December 1978

verheard

Chairman (of TV panel):
Oh, old Lord Braning tells a story about a reporter interviewing a woman who heard another woman shouting 'Please....! Don't....! STOP....!!!!' It appeared in the paper as 'Please don't stop'. (Laughs all round the studio.)

From a play *The Point of Balance?* by Donal Carroll

'When I was sent to a foreign country where there had been a rebellion my editor usually said that I should find somebody who had been raped!'

Christopher Hitchens ex-*Daily Express*, now *New Statesman*.

Topic 1 The Press

Read and discuss

(1) Do most papers support conservatism?
(2) What are the implications of this?
(3) What are the effects of many papers now being part of multinational concerns?
(4) Why do so few papers display their ownership 'with reasonable prominence'?
(5) Who owns your local paper? How would you find out? Is it stated on the paper?
(6) Is there a link between ownership and 'bias'?
(7) Define 'independent'. (Independent of what exactly?)
(8) Can a paper be independent?

Written work

(1) Compare various papers; what coverage is given to sport, advertising, politics etc?
(2) Analyse the way in which information (front page) is presented in two papers; one national, one local.
(3) Compare some of the leading views expressed in papers with the manifestoes of the three main political parties.
(4) Analyse in detail two articles (or editorials) which are attempting to persuade you but lack balance. What is the basis of their appeal? Could they only work in the absence of alternative means of information?
(5) Analyse the views, leading articles and editorials of four national papers. How similar are they?

Longer written work

(1) Does the popular press give people 'what they want'?
(2) Is there a contradiction between 'freedom of the press' and newspaper ownership? Can this give balanced coverage and reporting?
(3) Can papers *form* their readers' opinions? How adequate are they as sources of information?

THE PRESS

Table A Voting advice given by national daily newspapers and their % share of total daily shares

	June 1970	Oct 1974	Forecast for 1979 election
Daily Express	Con 24.6%	Con 21.1%	Con 17.2%
Sun	Lab 10.3%	all party coalition 23.7%	Con 28.2%
Daily Mail	Con 13.1%	Con-Lib 11.9%	Con 13.9%
Daily Mirror	Lab 32.1%	Lab 28.9%	Lab 27.1%
Daily Sketch	Con 5.5%	–	–
Daily Telegraph	Con 9.6%	Con 9.5%	Con 9.6%
Guardian	Lab-Lib 2.1%	more Lib influence 2.4%	probably Lab-Lib 2.0%
Times	Con-Lib 2.7%	Con-Lib 2.3%	Con or Con-Lib 2.1%

Notes
1. Source for 1970 and 1974 figures: *National Daily Papers and the Party System* HMSO 1977 quoted in Report of Royal Commission on the Press (Cmnd 6810 HMSO) Table 10.1
2. Source for 1979 circulation forecast: Audit Bureau of Circulations Statistics Jan-June 1978 (*British Rate & Data*).
3. *Financial Times* and *Morning Star* circulations are omitted from Royal Commission figures for 1970 and 1974 (see note 1). For comparability we have therefore left them out of the 1979 forecast.
4. No circulation figure for the new *Daily Star* was available as we went to press – though a figure of ¾ million is probable. The *Star* is owned by Trafalgar House.

Most of the national press — especially in the field of daily papers — is now operating in effect as a permanent propaganda organisation for the Conservative Party.

FOREIGN OWNERSHIP

Of the nine groups owning national newspapers, three are foreign-based multinational companies, three are foreign-conglomerates with substantial interests overseas. Only two Fleet Street proprietors are largely dependent on national newspapers published in this country.

The three overseas based groups are News International, the Observer and the Thomson Organisation.

Table B National newspapers in the UK: Sales (Jan-June 1978) and ownership

Dailies	Proprietor	Numbers sold
Sun	News International	3,930,554
Daily Mirror	Reed International	3,778,038
Daily Express	Trafalgar House	2,400,907
Daily Mail	Associated Newspapers Group	1,932,808
Daily Telegraph	Daily Telegraph	1,344,968
Times	Thomson Organisation	293,989
Guardian	Guardian & Manchester Evening News	273,201
Financial Times	S Pearson & Son	180,793
Sundays		
News of the World	News International	4,934,532
Sunday People	Reed International	3,853,561
Sunday Mirror	Reed International	3,832,394
Sunday Express	Trafalgar House	3,242,777
Sunday Times	Thomson Organisation	1,409,296
Sunday Telegraph	Daily Telegraph	844,589
Observer	Atlantic Richfield	688,458

Source Audit Bureau of Circulations (*British Rate & Data*)

The 1977 report of the Royal Commission on the Press investigated growing fears that political bias and multi-national ownership were squeezing diversity out of national newspapers. It decided these fears were misplaced. The Commission was, however in favour of 'wider public knowledge about the ownership of newspapers and periodicals.' The report made two interesting recommendations:

- that newspapers should print the name and address of the publisher, of their holding company (if any) and its location, and display both '*with reasonable prominence*'. The Commission suggested this information could be put beneath the newspaper title or on the leader page and '*not, as generally occurs at present, in minute print in an obscure position on the back page.* We recommend that the Press Council should police this obligation.' (Page 152, emphasis added)
- that newspapers should make a practice of declaring their interests when reporting or commenting on the affairs of an associated company or on an industry in which the publisher or an associated company has significant financial interests directly or indirectly. (Page 153).

The National press has totally ignored these recommendations. All daily newspapers continue to print the name and address of the publisher in minute type on the back page. Only one paper — the *Guardian* — publishes the name of its holding company and that is also in small type on the back page. The Press Council has done nothing at all to 'police' newspapers' compliance with this recommendation. Not one national newspaper makes a practice of declaring its interests when reporting on industries it has subsidiaries in.

Labour Research Department August 1979

(4) Does 'supporting conservatism' mean a higher profile for stories about personalities, Royalty, 'scroungers' etc? Does it imply a lack of balance and/or analysis?

(5) Can a mass circulation daily report politics in a meaningful way? (cf. *Daily Mirror*, 30 March) Does this type of reporting make politics more accessible? Does it make the policies of parties clearer?

'Freedom of the Press'

Spot the 'balance'

> Chief executive Victor Mathews is clear about the group's policy on newspapers, "It is very important in the present state of the country that the Beaverbrook papers should continue and express their views which are sympathetic to those of the Conservative Party and Capitalism" (*Financial Times* 1.7.77). Mathews was also reported as saying "By and large, the Editors will have complete freedom as long as they agree with the policy I have laid down" (*Financial Times* 1.7.77). Victor Mathews sits on the council of the Economic League. The group has donated £46,000 to the Conservative Party since 1976.

Labour Research Department March 1978

Maggie's poodle

The *Daily Mail* showed a touching concern for accuracy back in December. A National Opinion Poll survey, done for them, showed Labour with an 8 per cent lead over the Tories. The *Mail* worried that the result was "maverick." Naturally, they didn't want to misinform their readers and so gave no mention of Labour's lead; certainly no "Jim's on the right road" headlines.

This week NOP—using the same old methods—found the Conservatives 11 per cent in the lead. Carmelite House threw inconvenient doubts aside, and trumpeted "Maggie's got it right!" At least Lord Rothermere knows whose kennel he's in.

New Society 14 February 1978

It has been insufficiently remarked that not since Sir Harold Wilson's golden period, 1963-66, has any politician enjoyed quite so much support in the popular press. *Sun* and *Mail* bow down before her; nor is the *Express* altogether backward in its admiration.

We all know about the affecting relationship between Mrs Thatcher and Mr Larry Lamb, editorial director of Mr Rupert Murdoch's News International, which owns the *Sun* and the *News of the World*. I imagine that, were Mrs Thatcher Prime Minister, her good will would be invaluable if Mr Murdoch wished to acquire, say, *The Times* or the *Daily Telegraph*.

Mr Lamb's admiration is matched, maybe excelled, by that of Mr David English, editor of the *Daily Mail*. Mr English has several times refused to run cartoons by the distinguished artist, Mr John Kent, because they depicted Mrs Thatcher in a mildly unfavourable light.

Observer 28 May 1978

Topic 2   Turn your Radio on

Read and discuss

(1) Does local commercial radio give the people 'what they want'?
(2) Does advertising affect the quality or content of any programmes?
(3) Is local commercial radio real 'community' radio?
(4) Would it be any different if it was owned by the community?
(5) Does your local radio reflect the problems of the community? (and interests etc.)
(6) How analytical and balanced are the programmes?
(7) Could the various stations be compared with daily papers? (In London, for example, does Capital Radio=the *Sun*; Radio 4=the *Telegraph*?)
(8) *Phone-Ins*
Are they an example of real participation or of convenient cheapness? How balanced are they? (Are contributors simply allowed to air their prejudices including the chairperson?)

MASS COMMUNICATIONS

Labour Research Department August 1979

Commercial radio
Turn on, tune in, make profits

Local commercial radio was established under the Sound Broadcasting Act 1972, consolidated into the Independent Broadcasting Authority Act 1973. There are now 19 local stations, under the controlling authority of the Independent Broadcasting Authority. Five were set up in 1973, four in 1974, seven in 1975 and three in 1976. The IBA plans nine new stations with a target of 40 new stations

Profitability
The future growth of local commercial radio will not be solely in the interests of providing a public service though. Despite its initial slowness, ILR[1] has now become a profitable industry and for the first time figures for 1977-78 showed all 19 stations making a profit (see Table A). Big pickings in the London area have benefited music station Capital which increased profits by 66 per cent to £1.8 million last year, and even the once flagging LBC is beginning to show a profit. Glasgow's Radio Clyde has been the most profitable station, having paid a dividend to shareholders since its first year.

Total advertising revenue has more than trebled from £8.5 million in 1975 to £29.9 million in 1978.

At present about eight per cent of the total broadcasting output of the 19 stations is made up of adverts, still a distance from the maximum permissible of 15 per cent, that is nine minutes each hour.

Who owns local radio?
The 19 local radio stations currently operating are owned by consortia representing a variety of local interests rather than individual companies or persons. Local newspapers however, do play a major role in local radio ownership, a role encouraged by the Independent Broadcasting Authority Act 1973 which made provision for the IBA to give local newspapers the opportunity of acquiring shareholdings. Local press ownership now ranges from 14 per cent at Swansea Sound to 45 per cent of Thames Valley Broadcasting.

Capital 29.3 per cent owned by Dominfast Ltd, a private company in which Capital's directors (Bryan Forbes, Richard Attenborough etc) hold shares: 15 per cent by Rediffusion Radio Holdings, a subsidiary of British Electric Traction, which also owns half of Thames Television; 26 per cent by Local News of London, which produces 132 weekly papers in the London area; 12.2 per cent by the London *Evening Standard* and 8.9 per cent by the *Observer*.

LBC (London Broadcasting Co). Charterhouse Securities, part of the Charterhouse Group, owns 20 per cent; Associated Newspapers, which publishes the London *Evening News*, 16 per cent; Canadian-owned Selkirk Communications 12.5 per cent.

Piccadilly (Greater Manchester Independent Radio). 34 per cent owned by local papers including *Bolton Evening News* 11 per cent and *Manchester Evening News* 10 per cent; Manchester-based Granada Television 9 per cent.

Thames Valley (Reading) has the highest concentration of newspaper ownership: 45 per cent is owned by News International. Thames Television has 19.38 per cent, Windsor Racecourse 9.94 per cent and EMI 4.52 per cent. The EETPU owns 1.36 per cent. Tory Euro-MP and director Marquess of Douro owns 1.19 per cent.

Radio Orwell (Ipswich) is 15 per cent owned by Eastern Counties Newspapers, 15 per cent by EMI, 10 per cent by Anglia Television and 10 per cent by local co-operative society.

Table A Commercial local radio stations – turnover and profits

Contractor	Area	Turnover 1977-78 £000	& gain over 1976-77 %	Taxable profit 1977-78 £000	1976-77 £000	Potential VHF audience (000s)
Capital	London General	8319	+41.4	1865	1122	9160
LBC	London News	2469	+53.4	326	50	9160
Piccadilly	Manchester	2317	+23.6	600	462	2400
City	Liverpool	1631	+31.3	337	211	2000
Clyde	Glasgow	2559	+21.9	428	335	1900
BRMB	Birmingham	1700	+37.0	326	263	1700
Metro	Newcastle	1287	+32.2	182	91	1600
Beacon	Wolverhampton	912	+27.2	60	65	1240
Downtown	Belfast	not disclosed		73	55	975
Forth	Edinburgh	810	+22.7	98	20	930
Tees	Teeside	821	+27.7	101	91	680
Hallam	Sheffield	900	+33.7	153	99	660
Trent	Nottingham	750	+35.2	46	−30	600
Victory	Portsmouth	513	+26.0	27	−16	460
Pennine	Bradford	453	+17.1	22	36	400
Swansea Sound	Swansea	444	+25.8	61	36	320
Plymouth Sound	Plymouth	370	+19.0	44	39	280
210 Thames Valley	Reading	506	+37.9	74	41	270
Orwell	Ipswich	512	+28.6	41	−2	210

Source: *Investors Chronicle* 18.5.79

Who controls?

According to a survey by the Joint Industry Committee for Radio Audience Research in 1977, ILR now has an audience of 13·6 million adults. What access do these millions have to local radio? Minimal. Like most commercial enterprises, local radio is run by the directors in the interests of the shareholders, although, as we show here, these interests can range from purely business concerns to wider community and labour movement involvement.

Phone-in programmes offer very limited access: the independent Local Radio Workshop in a critical study of Capital Radio estimated "on current figures it would take a quarter of a century for 1–2 per cent of Londoners to speak for 2 minutes on Capital".[2] This study criticised Capital for little local input; excessive amount of commercial promotion (2 hours 23 minutes out of 13 hours); and non-compliance with the programme plans on which Capital's contract was awarded ie no drama, programmes on/for women, young people etc. The study reflects that "the only people who seem to benefit are the advertisers, the record companies and the shareholders".

Many of the stations are dominated by local business interests. Sometimes the business interests are of a national[3] or multinational character. But where co-operative and trade union bodies have participated in the consortia which have been awarded contracts there begins to be a greater reflection of the local community. Of the five new contracts awarded by the IBA,[4] Cardiff Broadcasting indicates a new approach for a local radio station. Half the board seats have been allocated to delegates of a Community Trust, and the interests of Welsh Women's Aid, South Wales Anti-Poverty Campaign, Freedom from Hunger Campaign and local youth and community projects are represented alongside religious, cultural and commercial interests.

All 19 local commercial radio stations are now making profits for their owners, who are still mainly local and national businesses

[1] *Independent Local Radio*

[2] *evidence submitted to the London Local Advisory Committee of the IBA, November, 1976*

[3] *The Royal Commission on the Press, 1977, reported that just five national companies (Thomson Organisation, Westminster Press – a subsidiary of S Pearson and Son – Associated Newspapers Group, United Newspapers, and Birmingham Post and Mail Holdings) own 52 daily and over 200 weekly newspapers*

[4] *For stations in Cardiff, Coventry, Dundee/Perth, Gloucester/Cheltenham and Peterborough*

Research work

Phone-Ins

(1) Tape or make notes on a local phone-in.
Do such programmes perform a public service for the sick, elderly, lonely etc?
Do they automatically exclude anybody without a phone?
List the number of contributions you agree/disagree with.
Are many contributions based on a lack of information?
What other form of mass communication is the source of information of many contributors? (Have copies of daily papers available.)
Should programmes have an educational responsibility?
Should phone-ins merely circulate opinions. Should the chairperson demand that people verify their assertions or identify their sources of information?
Is it possible to learn from phone-ins? Write up your conclusions.. Speculate on the role.

Radio Four: 'Any Questions'

(2) Tape or make notes. Analyse and evaluate.
Are contributions based on mere assertions? Are they backed up by facts and acknowledged sources? What is the response of the audience? How do the contributions compare with an average General Studies session?
What is the quality of the realisations? What paper would it compare with?
Write up conclusions. Speculate on the role of the programme.
(3) Monitor how local radio deals with community concerns: unemployment; housing etc.
(4) Compare '*Any Questions*' with a local radio phone-in.

Role play

Choose a controversial subject. Select an anchorman. Allow 2-minute contributions.

Labour Research Department August 1979

Visit

Arrange a visit to your local station. Ask producers what their purpose is. Make notes. Compare their purpose with their achievement. Is entertainment enough? Should they be attempting something more?

Topic 3   The *Star* – Porn or Pawn?

Read and discuss

(1) Is 'porn' the basis of appeal of some papers? (Compare a contemporary mass circulation paper with one of 10 years ago.)
(2) Is the appeal to the lowest common denominator?
(3) Do readers 'not want papers to be serious'? (cf. *Daily Mirror*, March 30.)
(4) Can papers raise circulation figures without page three girls?
(5) Would going 'full frontal' affect readership?
(6) How do the pictures in papers (the *Sun*, for example) affect quality and content? (The *Daily Mirror* quoted above had *no* naked women in it.)
(7) Compare the information with what you know. What are your sources of information? How did you get to know what you do know? Were papers useful? Which ones? How?

Written work

(1) *Mass circulation dailies*:
Analyse two in terms of sport, advertising, politics, 'scandal' coverage.
(2) Select two articles about women: Are they characterised by double entendres? Rewrite the article giving (a) the literal meaning, (b) any other meaning.
(3) Analyse three for items underneath the table. (cf. cartoon.) Compare the coverage of items above the table with those below.
(4) How would readers be *informed* if they were dependent on the mass-circulation press? (This could be related to phone-ins.)

'Not for cretins'.

The editors of the *Sun* and the *Daily Mirror* discussed their new rival, the *Star*, in the Radio 4 programme, *A Star is Born*. They both objected to the label 'down-market' for their type of newspaper.

Larry Lamb, of the *Sun*, said: 'I certainly run a newspaper which it's proper to call a working-class newspaper. It's impossible to sell four million copies and not do so. But to call the *Sun*, or for that matter the *Mirror*, "down-market" is to suggest that half the population of Great Britain is half-witted.

'I think there may very well be room for another newspaper. The best will survive, and I am quite determined that the *Sun* will remain the best. It will do better than anyone else what it sets out to do. Now, if the *Star* is setting out to do the same kind of thing, it causes me no anxiety at all, because it's clear from their public pronouncements that they don't understand what the *Sun* sets out to do, anyway.

'They don't begin to understand at Express Newspapers that the *Sun* is a serious newspaper. It's in deadly earnest. It pleases them to think that it's all racing and crumpet. As long as they are convinced of that, then we're in no danger at all.'

Mike Molloy of the *Daily Mirror* said: 'I don't think the *Mirror* has moved down-market in the last three years. I think it's a rotten term, "up-" or "down-market". We've made it more popular and, we hope, more readable and more interesting, but we're not pitching it at people whom we consider to be less intelligent than we previously thought they were.'

He felt that Express Newspapers, in promoting the *Star*, had shown 'contempt for their readers'.

'Jocelyn Stevens said that he was going to produce a paper with lots of tits and bums in it. The marketing director of the paper said that there's no magic about newspapers: it's like packaging beans and selling soap. That is an appalling attitude.'

George Scott said to Jocelyn Stevens: 'You will be familiar with the dictum of H. L. Mencken, the great American journalist, who said, in effect, that nobody ever lost money by underestimating the intelligence of the readership. Is that the way you are going to start out with the *Star*?'

Stevens said: 'Yes, we have no illusions about what we are doing. We believe that there is still a great market which the *Sun* is not getting. We are going to do what the *Sun* does—better.'

George Scott asked: 'Does that mean that you will outdo them in terms of titillation? More page-three girls? Or, will you have the first full-frontal in the daily newspapers?'

'That actually hasn't even been discussed—full frontal,' said Stevens. 'We may or may not. But certainly we are not going to shrink from pictures of girls not fully clothed. It is not going to be a *dirty* newspaper, it's—shall we call it "soft porn"? There is a mass audience which doesn't want newspapers to be serious.

'Politics will not be the main business of the *Star*. The paper will not have a fixed political viewpoint. It will sometimes come down on one side and sometimes the other. It is a genuine intention that the paper will only deal with politics when politics *interferes*, or becomes a matter of concern to the readers.'

George Scott said: 'The chairman of Express Newspapers, Victor Matthews, first had the idea of the new daily. Matthews, who is the undoubted boss of the newspaper group he took over some 18 months ago, has his own fairly strong political ideas, even if he doesn't always attach a party label to them.'

Victor Matthews said: 'I'm more interested in the circulation figures. If they're doing well with that, providing it's a responsible newspaper, I shan't interfere ...

We will support any party that really believes in the capitalist society, and I don't care what colour of politics they are. But, at the moment, this, basically, is the Conservative party.'

So will the *Star* be a paper the Express management can be proud of? Jocelyn Stevens said: 'This paper will not be for cretins. It'll be for young people who seek a provocative view of life, entertainment, news and sport. It will be one I shall be quite proud of.'

Victor Matthews looked more to the business side than the editorial content: 'My aim is to see a profit of something like £10 million a year from the Express group of newspapers. I've stuck my neck out, I could get egg all over my face and I could get the sack if my shareholders deem fit.

'I don't have ink in my veins. That side of it doesn't grip me as it does lots of people. But the challenge to make it a successful group is the satisfaction to me—provided we succeed.'

Victor Matthews: 'sticking his neck out'

The Listener 9 November 1978

Star over Bethlehem

the personal greetings card which Mr Peter Grimsditch, the editor of the new paper, the Daily Star, is sending to all his friends (from what I hear of the paper's sales it wouldn't have cost very much to send it to all his readers as well)

Longer written work

(1) Do mass communications create or reflect? Give examples.
(2) What is the role of papers like the *Sun/Star*? Do they divert attention from more serious issues? Do they trivialise and/or sensationalise? Do they act as 'consciousness-lowering'?

Research work

Examine the effect of new technology on the production of news.

Mass Communication — or Mass Deception

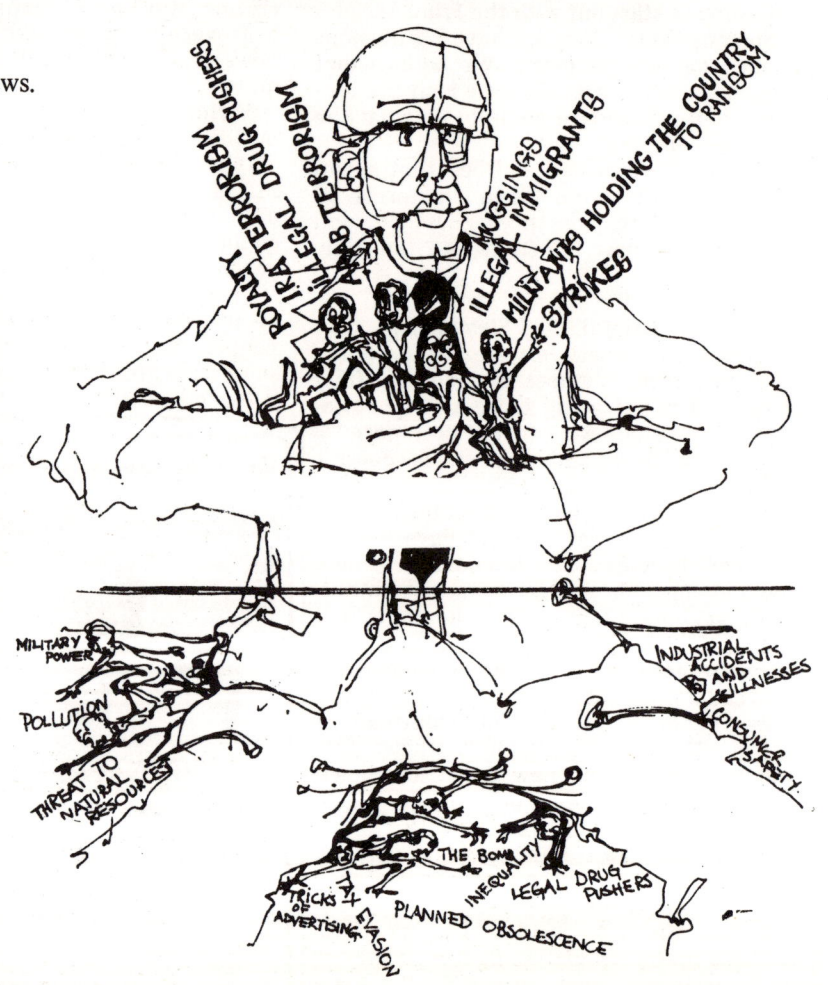

Inside story

THE NEW morning newspaper, the Daily Star, seems to be having trouble finding readers (possibly because there isn't much to read in it). But it never stops trying: in yesterday's edition there was a stirring story on the front page with the headline "Like Chris, you can be on a winner with the fantastic shooting Star."

The story told breathlessly how one "Chris Davis was thanking his lucky Star yesterday." It seems that Mr Davis read his horoscope in last Saturday's Star and it advised him to push his luck. So, for the first time in his life, Mr Davis gambled on the horses and won £367.

Given the facts in the Star, it was a truly wonderful story—and, given the facts the Star left out, it is a truly wonderful Diary item. For what the enthusiastic Star somehow omitted to mention ("pressure of space" was the reason I was given yesterday) is that lucky Mr Davis just happens to be the deputy night editor of the Daily Star. Well, I never.

Still, let's encourage the young Star. Yesterday's edition won the Diary award for the most tasteless story of the day (narrowly beating the Sun's drooling advice on how to take a girl's suspenders off). The Star story smacked its lips and told how "Respectable middle-aged ladies are being urged to pose topless for blue films. Invitations to bare all for the cameras will go out to 25,000 women next month."

Cor, wink, wink, pretty good story if you know what I mean. And then the Star tells us that "The films... are the latest form of screening for breast cancer."

Guardian 6 November 1978

Mirror Comment

Britain's paper Tories

EVERY daily newspaper in Fleet Street, except the Mirror and the Guardian, is Tory. Many of the staffs are not. Some of the editors are not.

But the proprietors are. And by tradition and instinct so are the papers.

To help those readers who take more than one paper at election times, the Mirror presents this brief sketch of its rivals.

THE SUN

THE SUN is owned by Australian Rupert Murdoch, who spends most of his time in New York. In 1970 it supported Harold Wilson **(lost)** and in 1974 Ted Heath **(lost again)**. Murdoch's Australian papers helped bring down the Labour Government there. The Sun is now one of Mrs. Thatcher's most fervent admirers.

The Daily Telegraph

THE DAILY TELEGRAPH is owned by Tory Lord Hartwell. Lady Hartwell's father was a Tory Cabinet Minister. So was the present editor, William Deedes. Its political editor, David Harris, was recently chosen as a Tory Euro-Candidate.

DAILY EXPRESS — THE VOICE OF BRITAIN

THE DAILY EXPRESS is owned by Trafalgar House and run by businessman Victor Matthews, a staunch Tory who only recently became involved with newspapers. **Last week it produced the silliest election stunt so far, by trying to show Labour and Communist policies were the same.** As silly as matching the Tory manifesto with the National Front's.

DAILY STAR

The Manchester **DAILY STAR** is a sick infant. Also from the Matthews stable, but so desperate for circulation it might support whichever party it thinks will be the most popular.

Daily Mail

THE DAILY MAIL is Fleet Street's Dirty Tricks specialist. **Known in the trade as the Tory Party's house magazine.** Its present proprietor, the 3rd Lord Rothermere, is a tax exile in France.

THE TIMES

THE TIMES is owned by Tory Canadian Lord Thomson, whose father was one of the last hereditary peers created by the Conservatives. Its editor is a twice-failed Conservative candidate.

THE GUARDIAN

THE GUARDIAN is Liberal by tradition and Labour by inclination (at least, most of its staff are). But owned by a trust and independent.

AND HOW ABOUT US?

DAILY Mirror

THE MIRROR is independent of all political groups but supports the re-election of Labour.

It is published by Mirror Group Newspapers, which is owned by Reed International Ltd. The chairman of Reed, Mr. Alex Jarratt, said on television the other day that "the Mirror has the enormous advantage of not having a proprietor."

Daily Mirror 17 April 1979

Can politics make the front page of a 'popular' daily in any meaningful way?

DAILY Mirror

Mirror Exclusive

Friday, March 30, 1979   8p

ON BEHALF OF MRS THATCHER, THE REPLY TO A PLEA FOR HELP!

By CHRIS HAMPSON

COUNCIL tenant Evelyn Collingwood was stunned by the letter she received from the office of Tory leader Margaret Thatcher.

Mrs. Collingwood had dropped a chatty note "to let Mrs. Thatcher know what ordinary people are thinking."

The reply she got, sent in the Tory Leader's name, came as a bombshell.

Mrs. Collingwood described it last night as "grossly insulting."

She said: "This letter makes out that all council house tenants are scroungers. Mrs. Thatcher must think we are all blooming peasants."

Mrs. Thatcher was upset, too. She said she hadn't known about Mrs. Collingwood's letter OR the reply.

Apology

And she sent a messenger with a hand-written apology to 53-year-old Mrs. Collingwood's home at Erith, Kent.

The letter to Mrs. Collingwood said:

● At Mrs. Thatcher's request I am replying on her behalf to your recent letter.

● I hope you will not think me too blunt if I say that it may well be that your council accommodation is unsatisfactory, but considering the fact that you have been unable to buy your own accommodation you are lucky to have been given something which the rest of us are paying for out of our taxes.

The letter was written on the Tory leader's headed House of Commons notepaper. It was signed by secretary Helen Senior on behalf of Mrs. Thatcher's Private Office aide Matthew Parris.

Mrs. Collingwood said last night: "It was a nasty reply."

Mrs. Collingwood, 49-year-old husband Fred and their daughter Marisa 22, live in a two-bedroom semi owned by Bexley council.

Mrs. Collingwood said: "I wrote to Mrs. Thatcher after seeing her talking on TV about buying council houses.

"I told her that some of us wouldn't want to buy our council houses even if we could afford to.

"I've got a nice little house, but the walls are so thin that we can hear next door's budgie pecking its seed!"

Mrs. Collingwood added: "I even said in my letter that I'd vote for her this time. I won't now."

I'M SO VERY SORRY..

THIS was how Mrs. Thatcher apologised last night:

● I was very upset indeed to read what was written on my behalf. I do not hold the views set out in that letter.

It was offensive and it lacked understanding of the views you express.

I can only apologise for the hurt it must have caused. Unfortunately, I cannot reply personally to the hundreds of letters which reach my office every day.

But each one should receive a courteous and attentive reply.

I am at a loss to think what happened in your own case.

HOUSE OF COMMONS
LONDON SW1A 0AA
6th March 1979

THE RT. HON. MRS. MARGARET THATCHER, M.P.

Dear Mrs Collingwood,

At Mrs Thatcher's request I am replying on her behalf to your recent letter.

I hope you will not think me too blunt if I say that it may well be that your Council accommodation is unsatisfactory, but considering the fact that you have been unable to buy your own accommodation you are lucky to have been given something, which the rest of us are paying for out of our taxes.

With good wishes,

Yours sincerely
Helen Senior

Matthew Parris
Private Office of the
Leader of the Opposition

Mrs Collingwood

BRUSH-OFF: The official letter that spelled trouble for the Tories and brought a hand-written note of apology from Margaret Thatcher.

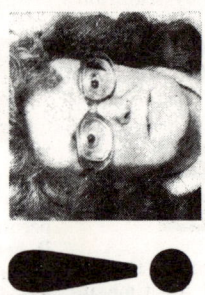

ANGRY: Mrs. Evelyn Collingwood yesterday

Mrs. Collingwood's Labour MP, James Wellbeloved, joined the attack.

He said the letter showed "the true Tory attitude" to council tenants.

Mrs. Collingwood's letter of apology from Mrs. Thatcher said she did not know how the blunder had happened. She told Mrs. Collingwood: "I am so very sorry."

Mrs. Collingwood's reaction: "I feel the apology is justified and I'm pleased Mrs. Thatcher was brave enough to own up."

UPSET: Mrs. T.

There were no naked women in this paper today.

Daily Mirror 30 March 1979

Topic 4 Television – Viewers' Droop?

Is the news neutral?

Read and discuss

(1) What is meant by 'balance'? Is equal *time* for each side sufficient to ensure it?
(2) What does Annan mean by 'broadcasters must share the assumptions of parliamentary democracy'?
(3) What are the 'accepted orthodoxies'?
(4) Why should the 'status and implications of the challenge' be made clear?
(5) How fairly are views critical of society at large or challenging to television coverage, reflected on television?
(6) Have you ever witnessed 'bias' on television?

Written exercises

(1) Record BBC News and ITV News. Compare coverage of the items above and below the table (cf. cartoon, p.78).
(2) Analyse any programme which has affected you and changed your way of thinking.
(3) Analyse some 'Open Door' programmes: (Southall; Racism) are they a 'challenge to accepted orthodoxies'?
(4) Write a letter of complaint to BBC/ITV about a programme you objected to. Write a letter of compliment about a television programme.
(5) Discuss the adequacy of television News as a source of information. (More than half the British electorate rely on television for their main supply of news.) (BBC Audience research, 1970)
(6) Write an interviewing script for any well-known personality. Ask awkward questions. Enact in class as a *role play*. (Or record if equipment available)

Research

Has the decline of British cinema (including attendance) got anything to do with the rise of television? (Further reading may be required.)

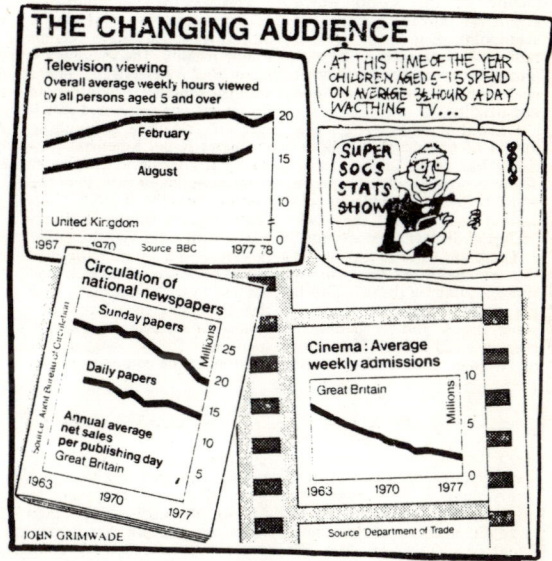

IS THE NEWS NEUTRAL?

One big difference between broadcasting organisations and newspapers in Britain is that the broadcasters are bound by law to be impartial, while newspapers are not.

It is fairly easy to spot the political colour of the various national newspapers, from the *Morning Star* (left-wing) to the *Daily Telegraph* (right-wing).

So, no-one is very surprised when newspapers, through their selection of news and the way they treat it, tend to present a picture of the world which supports their particular standpoint. But, with TV and radio it is supposed to be different. By law and convention, it is demanded they show "due impartiality."

Recently, however, the notion of broadcasters' impartiality has come under attack. There is now a body of opinion which believes that while broadcasters may *think* they are impartial, in fact they are not.

There are various versions of this argument, but they usually share a common thread. This is the charge that, by ignoring some issues, and by failing to present a full range of opinions on others, the media, while claiming to present a full and impartial picture of the world, are really presenting a narrow and distorted view.

One version of this argument stems from the theory that it is impossible ever to be perfectly impartial. According to this theory, our perception of the world is bound to be coloured by our own particular needs, experience, social class, culture, and so on. In news reporting, therefore, some degree of "cultural bias" is inevitable.

This was the standpoint of a recent controversial book attacking broadcasters' claims to impartiality. The sociological study *Bad News* (1976), opens with the sentence: "Contrary to the claims, conventions, and culture of television journalism, the news is not a neutral product." It goes on to analyse TV news bulletins broadcast in the first five months of 1975. Concentrating on industrial coverage, it concludes that the bulletins showed a "systematic presentation of a particular and narrow view . . . alternatives to this dominant view have little chance of surfacing in a meaningful way."

Some of the evidence quoted in *Bad News* is fairly startling. For example, during a long strike by dustcart drivers in Glasgow, of the 21 interviews broadcast, not one was with the strikers themselves.

This is a good example of the imbalance which can undoubtedly occur. The *Bad News* authors also make the point that "balance" is not simply a matter of both sides getting equal time. Even when that happens, the coverage may still be unbalanced if one side is presented in a more favourable way than another. Thus, in an industrial dispute, management may be presented in a better light than workers.

This was a point picked up by the Annan Committee in their *Report on the Future of Broadcasting* (1977): "Broadcasters too often forget that to represent management at their desks, apparently the calm and collected representatives of

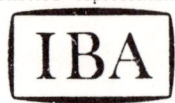

INDEPENDENT BROADCASTING AUTHORITY

order, and to represent shop stewards and picket lines stopping production, apparently the agents of disruption, gives a false picture of what strikes are about."

Annan, however, rejected the charge that broadcasters were guilty of deliberate and calculated bias, preferring simply to call the coverage of industrial affairs "in some respects inadequate and unsatisfactory."

But what about the larger assertion that "TV news is not a neutral product"? The Annan report has a good deal to say on this general subject. Its arguments are subtle and turn on the fact that what is demanded from broadcasters is not simply "impartiality" but *due* impartiality." A good deal of significance attaches to that word "due."

According to Annan, "due impartiality" is not the same as "neutrality." In some areas, broadcasters are specifically expected *not* to be neutral: "The broadcasters are operating within a system of parliamentary democracy and *must* share its assumptions. They should not be expected to give equal weight or to show an impartiality which is not due to those who seek to destroy it by violent, unparliamentary or illegal means." (italics added)

So, terrorists are out. And not only terrorists. The Independent Broadcasting Authority (IBA), the governing body of commercial broadcasting, says quite clearly in its TV *Programme Guidelines* (1978): "The Authority is not required to secure impartiality on matters such as drug-trafficking, cruelty and racial intolerance, for example, on which society, even today, is virtually unanimous."

What this means is that "due impartiality" is, in effect, impartiality *within a defined area*. The theory is that society has reached a consensus—a broad

BRITISH BROADCASTING CORPORATION

general agreement—on some questions: for example, that drug trafficking should be opposed, or that parliamentary democracy is the best form of government for this country. It is the duty of broadcasters to reflect this consensus. But in other areas, consensus has not been reached. Here the broadcasters must act impartially, providing a platform on which issues can be fully debated.

But even within this second area, broadcasters are not expected to give equal weight to every opinion. As Annan puts it: "Broadcasters must take account, not just of the whole range of views on an issue, but also of the weight of opinion which holds these views. Their duty to let the public hear various voices does not oblige them to give too much weight or coverage to opinions which are not widely held. *While it is right that the accepted orthodoxies should be challenged, equally it is essential that the established view should be fully and clearly put and that the status and implications of the challenge should be made clear*." (italics added)

It does seem inevitable that some people are going to be unhappy with the "due impartiality" granted them. Small political parties, for example, are not often going to get their voice on the air. From their point of view the system is going to seem very unfair. A minority political party which believes the media are biased against it, may well also believe that this is one reason why the party remains a minority: how can it grow when it is denied the chance to counter the arguments against it constantly broadcast by the media? The media, on the other hand, may say they are merely making a realistic and democratic assessment of the political reality: why *should* they give equal weight to the views of a party which consistently fails to win votes?

The fact that the media may tend to reflect the status quo does not mean they are unaware, however, that the status quo itself changes over time. Annan points out that: "the range of views and the weight of opinion are constantly changing. What may be an acceptable and justifiable approach to an issue at any one time will not necessarily remain so for all time." This is clearly true. The question is: how big a part do the media play in shaping the public's view of the acceptable approach, and how much is the public's view of what is acceptable reflected by the media? Do the media lead? Or are they led? Does the power lie with the media? Or with their audience?

This affects not just questions of party politics but also of taste. Nudity, for example, is not uncommon on TV today. Yet only ten years ago it would have been unthinkable. Has TV created the taste for nudity among its viewers? Or is it able to show nudity because that is what its viewers now want? (The two things could, of course, be inter-connected.)

And what about those who find nudity distasteful? Mrs Mary Whitehouse's National Viewers' and Listeners' Association, for example, would like to see a lot less nudity on TV. Are the broadcasters biased against them? Or are they showing "due impartiality" in assuming their views are not widely held?

To say TV news is not neutral is less a criticism than a statement of the obvious. The views of certain groups (terrorists, racists, etc) are specifically excluded from the broadcasting arena. And within that arena, more weight is given some groups' opinions than others'. This is not neutrality. Nor, in the strict sense, is it impartiality. "*Due* impartiality" it may well be. But whether you feel that is a reasonable principle, reasonably acted upon, may well depend on the degree of due impartiality the media extend to your own point of view.

Sight and Sound Spring 1977

Subject Area: Political Literacy

The nature of modern British politics with reference to the contemporary political spectrum; identification of various parties and groups; the basis of their appeal and the concepts underpinning their beliefs; the distribution of income and wealth.

Aims

(1) To extract and interpret information and evidence.
(2) To locate and analyse sources of reference.
(3) To recognise the relevant aspects of an argument and determine the implications.
(4) To organise information through basic political concepts and generalisations.
(5) To develop a role for the application of reasoning to problems.
(6) To make explicit and defend one's own assumptions.
(7) To participate effectively in a group, recognising one's effect on others.

Part of the overall teaching aim is to make politics more accessible.

Topic 1   Politics, what politics?

Initial exercise
As briefly as you can, write down what you think the term 'right wing' means. Write down what you think is meant by 'left wing'.

Discuss and compare.

Now examine 'Left–Right–Centre'. (Be as *critical* as possible.)
(1) How adequate is this as a description of modern political geography?
(2) Are there additions you would make? Deletions?
(3) How do these ideas relate to how you have heard them in mass communications?

Design exercise

This will involve some research, possibly project-type work.
Draw up your own political map.
Consult the manifestoes of *all* the groups if necessary.

LEFT	CENTRE			RIGHT
	(mixture)			
Collective ownership of the means of production				Concentration of wealth, power and control in the hands of the few
Nationalisation (without compensation)				More money on arms and 'private enterprise'
				Military service
Redistribution of wealth: implying elimination of unemployment, homelessness		Labour Party	Tory Party	
Opposition to private medicine, education and other welfare services		Liberal Party		Increasing restriction of civil liberties
Allocation of resources based on need rather than ability to pay	Communist Party		National Front National Party	Capital punishment
Planned economic system	International Marxist Group			Competition
Cooperation	Socialist Workers' Party			Economic 'free market'
Greater emphasis on environmental factors in explaining human activity	Workers Revolutionary Party			Greater emphasis on genetic factors in explaining human activity
(In varying degrees, some of these elements would come under the heading of Socialism.)				(In varying degrees, some of these elements would come under the heading of Fascism.)

Most political parties, particularly the three main ones should be seen as containing a mixture of tendencies.

POLITICAL LITERACY 85

> **'Social reformer for some appears to be a dirty phrase'**
>
> JAMES CAMERON faces the music

> Dr Edward Norman, you will remember, argued at great length that Christians were wrong to concern themselves with matters of temporal and mortal concern, and that the Church is in error when it encourages them to do so. It was the old theorem that religion must not get involved with politics.
>
> There is a great deal to be said for this view, if you interpret "politics" in the tiresome contemporary sense of party groupings and alignments. My reading of the word is quite different: polls, politics, the study of the organisation of society. And if Jesus Christ was not profoundly concerned in that then what was his point?
>
> If I may give news to this correspondent, there are no timeless or ultimate values that are subject to me, which is a good thing for the world. Then he gives the game away, with my "prevailing views of social morality." If he knows what those are he is wiser than I, for they change all the time. Then comes the clincher: Christians must not align themselves with politicians, "be they Wedgwood Benns or Robert Mugabes."
>
> Who was it said that the Christian church is the Tory Party at prayer?
>
> I am denounced for suggesting that Christ was concerned in political matters, or as far as that could be defined in the Palestine of his day, because the critics define politics in the simplistic meaning of today — the hustings, the charade of Westminster, the confrontations on television. Obviously Christ would have avoided these mean things. But with my back to the wall I still insist that "politics" means the organisation of man's relationship to man, and that was what Christ was on about.
>
> Thus he was put to a political trial and suffered a political death in company with others who had offended against the law of the land. To deny him that right is, I think, to deny the historical Jesus's right to be remembered at all.

Guardian December 1979

Write down
(1) What you think is meant by the term 'politics'.
(2) Areas of your life you think are affected by politics/areas you think are not.

Now read the article.
(1) How adequate is his definition?
(2) How does it compare with yours?
(3) Does this mean *everything* is political?

List aspects of your life which you think you do not control.

List those you think you do control.

Who controls those outside your influence? (if any)

Topic 2 Wealth/Poverty: Income/Outcome

Read and discuss

(1) Are these examples exceptional? Include any other examples you are aware of.
(2) How are the sums of money the musicians spent earned? Are the musicians overtaxed?
(3) Do they *need* more?
(4) Are there any moral or political implications in how their money is spent?
(5) Can the pursuit of luxury be justified?
(6) Can being a 'tax exile' be justified?

Mick's nose for the hard stuff

EX - ROLLING STONE Mick Taylor has had to undergo surgery on his nose as a result of his propensity for sniffing cocaine, I can reveal today.

Taylor — who vanished soon after quitting the Stones five years ago—so damaged the membrane between his nostrils that it has had to be partially replaced with a piece of plastic.

Taylor developed his taste for a nose full of white powder while with the Stones — a band who discovered early in life that things go better with coke.

Now that his nose has healed, Taylor is making a bid to return to the music scene with a solo album.

Evening News August 1979

● The new owner of Who drummer Keith Moon's country house was surprised to find its glass wall shattered and a Rolls-Royce Corniche standing in the swimming pool, where it had evidently reposed for some years. These, however, were only the later incidents in the eccentric life of 'Mad' Moon, whose penchant for destruction can be traced back to an American tour by The Who, when $30,000-worth of damage was done to a Holiday Inn in celebration of Moon's 21st birthday. In those days, he used to carry a hatchet around in his personal luggage for such moments: once, in Saskatoon, Canada, he felt bored and chopped up everything in his hotel-room: the bed, the cupboards, the chairs and the television set.

On another occasion, Moon's accountant informed him that he was a millionaire, and that he should spend some of the money to avoid paying excessive tax on it. In six weeks Moon spent all of it, buying four houses, eight cars, an hotel, a riverside bungalow and, finally, a watch costing £2000 (which stopped soon afterwards).

POLITICAL LITERACY 87

Jackie 'could be £15,000 in red'

JACQUELINE ONASSIS — faces changes in her lifestyle.

NEW YORK, Wednesday.
JACQUELINE KENNEDY ONASSIS may enjoy income of about 350,000 dollars (about £175,000) next year, but she could find herself in the red to the tune of some 30,000 dollars (about £15,000), according to a financial analysis published today.

According to Money magazine, Mrs Onassis, widowed for the second time when her Greek shipping tycoon husband Aristotle Onassis died in Paris earlier this year, now faces some changes in her lifestyle and important financial decisions.

Basing its analysis of her income and spending on published records, the magazine said that next year she will collect 100,000 dollars (£50,000) from a tax-exempt, pre-nuptial trust set up by Mr Onassis, 100,000 dollars (£50,000) of taxable income from his will, 37,050 dollars (£18,500) from the estate of former U.S. President John Kennedy, 4160 dollars (£2080) from the estate of her father, John Vernon Bouvier and 200 dollars (£100) a week from her job as an associate editor at a publishing house.

And if she successfully negotiates for a bigger slice of the Onassis fortune, she could gain another 100,000 dollars (£50,000).

Although her total wealth was estimated at 14.4 million dollars (£7,200,000), the magazine described her financial position as "asset rich and cash poor."

It said that her spending was estimated at 381,000 dollars (£190,000) a year—or 30,000 dollars (£15,000) more than she has coming in.

Among her current expenses, the magazine listed:

100,200 dollars (£50,100) for income tax; 85,000 dollars (£42,500) for staff and servants; 50,000 dollars (£25,000) for home decoration and renovation; 10,000 dollars (£5000) for clothes; 10,000 dollars (£5000) to maintain her Fifth Avenue apartment in New York; 10,000 dollars (£5000) for entertainment;

The magazine said Mrs Onassis spent up to 120,000 dollars (£60,000) a year on clothes when Mr Onassis was alive—but has cut down lately—and 30,000 dollars (£15,000) for clothes could be "on the skimpy side." (Reuter)

Evening Standard 24 September 1975

"Rolling Stone Mick Jagger has been ordered to pay his estranged wife £1,500 a week maintenance. 'That's what she needs – and that's what she'll get' said a Los Angeles judge. Apart from living expenses, including hotel bills of up to £13,000 a month, "I still owe money to Christian Dior and Yves St Laurent" said Bianca Jagger. (*Daily Express* 9.6.79)

Everything is what it is only by contrast

Below the poverty line

By our Labour Staff

One family in eight in Britain was living on or below the official poverty line at the end of 1977, according to the latest report from the Low Pay Unit.

On a more liberal definition of poverty, one person in four was poor in 1977, Mr Field claims. This figure, representing 14 million people in 7.6 million families, is of those who earned up to 40 per cent above the supplementary benefit line.

The supplementary benefit level is officially acknowledged to afford a very poor standard of living, Mr Frank Field, the unit's former director, now Labour MP for Birkenhead, says. The Supplementary Benefits Commission told the Royal Commission on the Distribution of Income and Wealth that the scheme provided, particularly for families with children, "incomes that are barely adequate to meet their needs."

His report, based on the Department of Health and Social Security's Family Expenditure Survey for December 1977, says 2.02 million people were living on incomes below the supplementary benefit level and 4.16 million were receiving supplementary benefits.

There is nothing in Conservative policy to lead one to expect anything but a substantial increase in the numbers of poor in coming years, Mr Field says.

One in Eight: A Report on Britain's Poor. Low Pay Unit.

Compare the examples of poverty.

(1) Can poverty be justified?
(2) Is there any relation between poverty and wealth?
(3) How could poverty be eliminated?
(4) Is 'poverty' simply a financial concept?

Research work

Find out by either visiting or writing to your local Department of Health and Social Security office what the contemporary Government definition of 'poverty' is.

A report from the Low Pay Unit estimated that one in four of the British population were living in households with incomes below or near the poverty line. The report also said that in 1976 290,000 full-time workers were getting less at work than they would have been getting on the dole. (*Morning Star* 5.9.78)

A young mother who stole a coat in a plan to buy a pram for her 11 months old baby was told by magistrates: "You must realise that there are things in the world which we cannot afford to buy". The 17 year old woman, who was living on social security, was fined £25. (*South London Press* 11.8.78)

A report from the Low Pay Unit says that most of Britain's 250,000 homeworkers earn less than 40p an hour, and almost a fifth get less than 10p an hour, "fewer than half of the homeworkers earned more than £10 a week despite sometimes working more than 50 hours a week. A survey disclosed that two workers knitting at home earned £1·62 and £2·25 for working 48 and 60 hours respectively." (*Times* 4.7.78)

A family living in a council home in Cornwall dumped their new born baby at an electricity board office in protest at having their electricity cut off four times in 14 months. The father said "we were at our wits end. We had just a couple of candles for lights and a gas burner for cooking. How can you keep a small baby warm on that?" He admitted owing £190 in electricity bills, but the house is fitted with expensive central heating, costing about £70 a quarter. "My take-home pay is only £38 a week. You just can't run our sort of heating with that sort of money." (*Daily Mail* 9.2.79)

Sir Charles Clore has made £20 million from the sale of 16,627 acres in Hertfordshire. He lives abroad, and the sale will not be subject to capital gains tax. He is also trying to sell a 1,250 acre Berkshire estate for £4 million. "The Clore fortune is estimated at more than £50 million". (*Daily Mail* 31.5.79)

Property man John Sunley bought seven bedroomed Heath House, Hampstead for £400,000 last April. Without ever living there, he sold it in July for £625,000. The Saudi buyer put the house back on the market in August – at a new price of £2 million. (*London Evening Standard* 17.8.78)

GEC boss Sir Arnold Weinstock has bought a £2·5 million executive jet for his company. The Grumman Gulfstream 11 does two miles to the gallon. (*Daily Mail* 11.6.79)

"Lord Croham, less than a year after retiring as head of the home Civil Service, has been appointed a part-time deputy chairman of the British Oil Corporation. He will spend the equvalent of two days a week at his new job and will get £10,000 a year – about £100 for each day's work .... he is already an industrial adviser to the Bank of England and also collects a Civil Service index-linked pension of about £9,350 a year." (*Daily Mail* 2.9.78)

A boss has given himself a £4,080 a week pay rise. Norman Castle's last salary as chairman of S & W Berisford leapt 350 per cent, from £60,500 to £272,672 – a rise of £212,172. (*Daily Express* 19.2.79)

Dare you eat your fish fingers off anything else? Mintons have produced a bone china and 24 carat burnished gold dinner service. "A cup and saucer – or a single plate – costs £177·85; a soup tureen will set you back as much as a Mini. If you have around £50,000 you can own a full splendid dinner service for 24". And to complement the china, how about sterling silver cutlery from Aspreys – a one place setting costs £389·45, for 12 £8,115. And a French cotton voile tablecloth and napkins, embroidered with metallic gold thread, for £320. (*Daily Mail* 8.6.78)

"At Sotheby's yesterday a bottle of Chateau d'Yquem 1858, an outstanding year for Sauternes, sold for £665." (*Guardian* 23.5.79)

A dance at the Cafe Royal was recently put on by Lord Brooke, who made £3 million from the sale of Warwick Castle and its contents. The do, for 800 guests, cost more than £30,000 (*Daily Mail* 5.6.79)

Topic 3 Who owns Britain? Distribution of wealth and income.

Read and discuss

(1) Define 'income'.
(2) Define 'wealth'.
(3) Why are income and wealth kept separate?

WHAT DO WE MEAN BY INCOME AND WEALTH?

Income = receipts from work or investment

Wealth = the financial or other assets a person or organisation possesses

Income has always been kept separate from *wealth* in the taxation system in this country.

"It is obviously important that the inter-relationships between the income and wealth of individuals should be studied. For example, the role of inheritance in relation to income levels and wealth holdings is a matter for investigation. Unfortunately, however, the official statistics of personal income and wealth do not enable such relationships to be established."
(The Royal Commission, Standing Reference, para. 52)

The Royal Commission on Taxation in its 1955 Report said that a definition of income for taxable purposes should include all that constitutes "the net accretion of economic power between two points of time." In other words the *wealth* that a person has acquired between two points of time, as well as the *income*. If the Government accepted this then it is most unlikely that income alone would continue to be tightly taxed on a PAYE basis, whilst wealth escapes tax except when it is transferred upon death.

Rigid separation

The rigid separation of income from wealth for taxation purposes, together with the absence of major sources of data on income and wealth other than the Inland Revenue, means that we do not know much about the true situation, i.e. about who really owns the wealth, and unfortunately the official statistics do not help much either. That is because official statistics are always the product of the system as it exists. The official statistics in this case retain the traditional distinction between income and wealth, that is needed for the collection of taxes. Also the statistics are only as accurate as the Inland Revenue's ability to harness tax evasion, and everyone knows how imperfect that can be.

There are two other sources of information on the distribution of income (but not wealth): the Family Expenditure Survey and the New Earnings Survey, but neither of them can be compared directly with the Inland Revenue data. This is because the Inland Revenue figures are based on *tax units*, i.e. single persons or married couples, whereas the Family Expenditure Survey is based on *families* and the New Earnings Survey only on *individuals*. Similarly, and this is very significant, all the data that exists on wealth is based on individuals. If wealth is passed around the family in order to avoid tax liability, this process will show up in the official statistics in the form of a trend towards greater equality in the ownership of wealth! — in other words, precisely the opposite of what it really is.

Initial exercise

Draw up a national pay table: Who would be at the top/bottom?

Select 20 types of job, including a managing director and a dustman.

Take these factors into account:
> Responsibility; job satisfaction; status; reward other than income; qualifications; monotonous work; career structure/lack of career structure; social usefulness; prospects etc.

Consider also factors which *prevent* people getting more satisfying jobs.

Compare and discuss.

Read and discuss

(1) What are the statistical inequalities of income?
(2) Is financial 'income' an adequate definition for everything some employees receive from work?
(3) Has there been any improvement by the lower paid in terms of the average wage? Why/why not?

Discussion points leading to written work

(1) Should we all try to get all we can, financially?
(2) Do we have any larger responsibilities?
(3) *Incentives*: Do those with more responsibility need more/deserve more?
Do those in unskilled work deserve more/need more?
(4) Should there be a maximum wage *and* a minimum wage? What opposition would either meet?

This could be organised as a *debate*.

Two speakers for either side with adequate time to prepare.

Rest of group take notes and make smaller contributions later in debate.

INCOME

The facts on income

The situation, as far as income from employment is concerned, has also received a lot of attention recently. The new earnings survey for April 1975 shows that 80 per cent of full-time adult male workers earned between £37.50 and £88.20 per week with a middle wage of £55.90. The highest paid managers in industry received £50,000 per year and more, which is 17 times the middle or 25 times the wages of the bottom 10 per cent of full-time adult male workers. In 1974/5 there were 64,000 people earning more than £10,000 or £192 per week, and 2,500 earning £24,000 or more, or £461 per week.

Income

Trade union policy on income distribution rather than income relationship has been concerned with the overall range of incomes.

NUPE has recently suggested a National Maximum Wage, beyond which income tax would be levied at a rate of 100 per cent. Commenting on this idea the Government has said that this would only yield an increase in revenue of about 6 per cent, but NUPE point out that 6 per cent would mean an increased yield to the Exchequer of £728 million each year.

'This would be sufficient to take a substantial number of low-paid workers out of the income tax net, or alternatively to increase the funding of the National Enterprise Board by 75 per cent, or triple the hospital building programme'.

NUPE Economic Review, 'Time for a Change'

Earning power is still heavily concentrated in the hands of those on the top salaries. In 1976-77 the top 2 per cent of income earners (those on over £10,000 a year) shared between them almost 9 per cent of all personal incomes, and the top 20 per cent (on over £5,000 a year) cornered 40 per cent (*Inland Revenue, Surveys of Personal Incomes, 1975-76 and 1976-77;* and *Inland Revenue Statistics 1978,* HMSO £5.00 and £4.75 respectively).

Inequality of incomes

Total income

The top 10% of income-earners get about a quarter of all total income: and so do the bottom 50% of all income-earners.
(Royal Commission on the Distribution of Income and Wealth, Standing Reference, para. 318)

No progress

1886: 68.6% of average earnings
1960: 70.6%
1975: 69.2%
LOWEST PAID 10%

In 1975 the lowest paid 10% of men doing manual jobs earned 69.2% of average earnings; in 1960 the figure was 70.6%, and back in 1886 it was 68.6%.
(PIB Report 169, and New Earnings Survey 1975)

The Royal Commission looked at higher incomes over £10,000 a year but the self-employed were not included at all and the Commission acknowledged the serious lack of information about fringe benefits.

WEALTH

Read and discuss

(1) What are the statistical inequalities of total wealth?
(2) What are the inequalities in relation to shares and property?
(3) Why is wealth so concentrated?
(4) Should there be a wealth tax? What opposition would it meet?

The Distribution of Wealth
based on figures from the Royal Commission on the distribution of income and wealth

'Many social commentators have argued in recent years that the problems of extreme inequality have been solved by taxation and that there are no longer any super-rich people. The reports of the Royal Commission... show otherwise. The total amount of privately held wealth in the U.K. in 1973... is estimated to have been £213 billion. This is about 75 per cent of the net wealth of the whole country, with the Government, companies, and overseas residents owning the rest... 28.1 per cent of all this wealth is held by 1 per cent of the adult population and 53.9 per cent by 5 per cent. The bottom 80 per cent of the adult population holds 17.6 per cent of all private wealth'.
TUC Economic Review, 1976

Trade Union Studies, BBC Publications

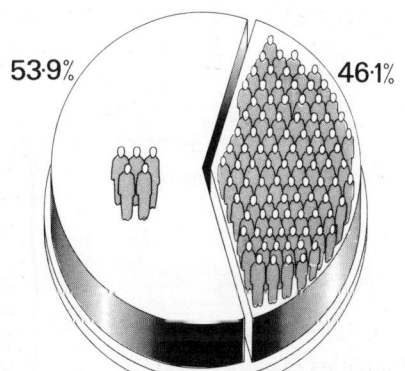

The National Cake:
out of every 100 people the five richest own more of the wealth than the remaining ninety five.

Director	Company	Value of shareholding at June 1, 1973 £m
Lord Thomson	Thomson Organisation	59.5
Sir Jules Thorn	Thorn Electrical Industries	29.6
Sir Charles Forte	Trust Houses Forte	28.9
Lord Samuel	Land Securities Investment Trust	28.0
Sir Godfrey Mitchell	George Wimpey & Co	20.0
Lord Pilkington	Pilkington Brothers	15.9
Maxwell Joseph	Grand Metropolitan Hotels	10.6
Hyman Kreitman	Tesco Stores (Holdings)	10.0

from *The 2 Nations: Inequality in Britain*

Wealth In its 1976 Economic Review the TUC argues that a high priority should be given by the Government to developing a wealth tax. but it may be worth adding some further figures at this point. The reports of the Royal Commission on the distribution of Income and Wealth show that the top 0.1 per cent own 12 per cent of privately owned wealth. The top group (about 31,000 individuals) each have estates worth a minimum of £200,000. The bottom 50 per cent of the adult population (16.5 million individuals) are estimated to have an average of £700. The super-rich own 30.8 per cent of all privately owned Government securities, 36.9 per cent of all privately owned quoted company shares, 38.7 per cent of all other privately owned company securities and 42.2 per cent of all privately owned land. The top 3.5 per cent of the adult population own 90 per cent of all privately owned quoted company shares and 91 per cent of all privately owned land in the U.K.

Written work

(1) Why is wealth more concentrated than income?
(2) How is wealth maintained?

Research work (for possible *project*)

What other inequalities are there? Do they relate to inequalities of income and wealth?

Longer written work

(1) Define 'inequality'. Has it anything to do with politics?
(2) Are there any social implications in inequalities of income and wealth? What are they?
(3) Are there any connections between wealth and poverty? (cf. 'contrast' sheet)

The wealthiest 1% in Britain hold four-fifths of all personally-held company shares. A.B. Atkinson in his analysis of the portfolios of the rich, writes. 'The top 1% appear to own four-fifths and the top 5% nearly all the company shares which are owned directly by the personal sector.' (*Unequal Shares* p31). Apart from benefitting from the income and wealth 'the wealthy shareholder may well be in a position to exercise considerable influence over a company's policy, and in a substantial number of cases the owners retain full control.' (pp43-4)

POLITICAL LITERACY 93

Topic 4 Paying through the tax system

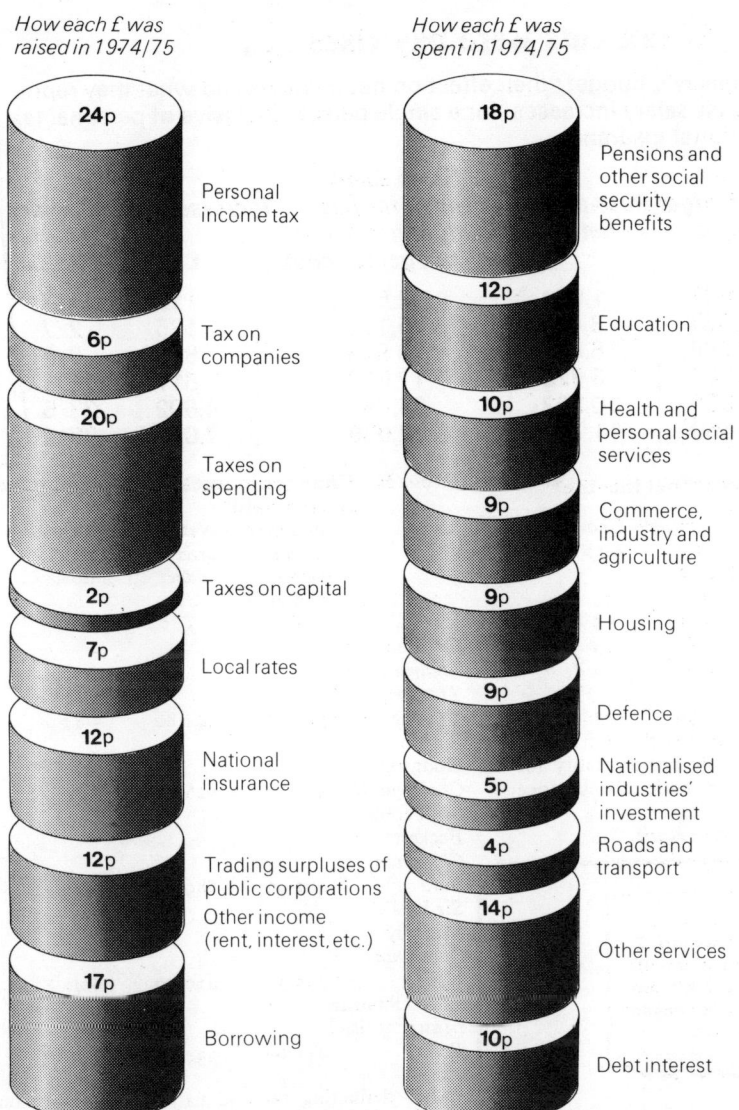

How each £ was raised in 1974/75

- 24p Personal income tax
- 6p Tax on companies
- 20p Taxes on spending
- 2p Taxes on capital
- 7p Local rates
- 12p National insurance
- 12p Trading surpluses of public corporations / Other income (rent, interest, etc.)
- 17p Borrowing

How each £ was spent in 1974/75

- 18p Pensions and other social security benefits
- 12p Education
- 10p Health and personal social services
- 9p Commerce, industry and agriculture
- 9p Housing
- 9p Defence
- 5p Nationalised industries' investment
- 4p Roads and transport
- 14p Other services
- 10p Debt interest

Trade Union Studies, BBC Publications

Overheard

Prime Minister: What I really need is a one-handed Chancellor!
M.P.: Whatever for?
P.M.: Well, then I'll have an economist who can make decisions.
M.P.: How come?
P.M.: He can't say 'Well on the one hand... and on the other hand'....

Before tax 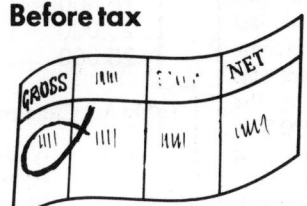   **After tax**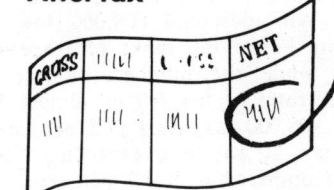

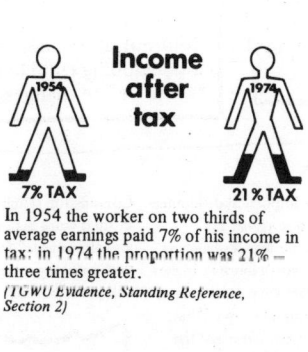

Income after tax

In 1954 the worker on two thirds of average earnings paid 7% of his income in tax; in 1974 the proportion was 21% — three times greater.
(TGWU Evidence, Standing Reference, Section 2)

Tax liability 1954–1974

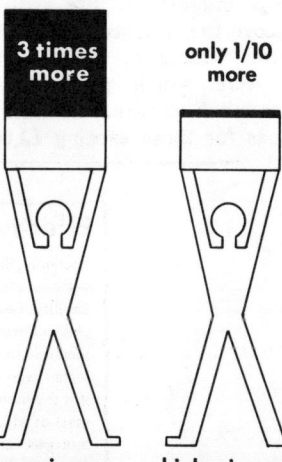

3 times more — lower income bracket

only 1/10 more — higher income bracket

Tax burden shifts to poor

In the last decade, the burden of direct taxation has increasingly shifted from companies and the wealthy to income tax payers. The amount of revenue contributed by companies and their shareholders has fallen from 21 per cent of the total receipts collected by the Inland Revenue (basically direct as opposed to indirect taxes) in 1968-69 to just 17 per cent this year. The yield from wealth taxes (estate duty and capital transfer tax) has also fallen, from 6 per cent to 1 per cent. Meanwhile, the income tax payers' contribution has increased from 66 to 78 per cent.

Within the income tax sector, there have been significant shifts in the burden of taxation from rich to poor in the last year. An additional 600,000 low income earners joined the ranks of taxpayers this year, while the numbers subject to the higher rates of tax *fell* by almost 300,000. Only 808,000 taxpayers (3.8 per cent) now pay tax at anything exceeding the basic rate (compared with 5.3 per cent in 1977-78). Allowances and reliefs, which are of disproportionate benefit to the rich, reduced total taxable income by 40 per cent. Mortgage interest and life assurance relief alone cost the Exchequer £1,400 millions this year. Mortgage interest and similar reliefs were worth proportionately four times as much to taxpayers earning £20,000 a year as for those earning £2,000.

The budget and take home pay

If tax cuts were pay rises . . .

Amendments to Healey's budget: their effect on net incomes and what they represent in terms of gross salary increases, for a single person, inclusive of personal tax allowance and national insurance.

Salary	Pre-budget net pay	Post-budget net pay	Gross salary needed for post-budget net pay at pre-budget tax rates	Increase in gross salary £	%
2,500	1,827	1,904	2,617	117	4·7
5,000	3,334	3,423	5,135	135	2·7
10,000	6,266	6,607	10,816	816	8·2
15,000	8,208	8,929	17,517	2,517	16·8
20,000	9,555	10,503	24,692	4,692	23·5
25,000	10,560	11,752	32,039	7,039	28·2

Table A Changes in weekly net income*

Gross pay £	Net income before budget** £	Net income after budget £	Change in net income %
60	54·47	57·29	+5·2
100	78·67	82·69	+5·1
200	143·47	150·42	+4·8
300	191·00	211·43	+10·7
400	230·45	262·59	+13·9

*Assumes married man with two children under 11 (or single person with sole responsibility for children) after deducting tax, national insurance and including child benefit.
**Also before changes agreed in April.

Table B Changes in weekly net income for the top paid*

	Net weekly income before budget** £	Net income after budget £	Change in net income per cent
C C Pocock† *Chairman Shell Transport and Trading*	511·50	944·80	+84·6
Sir Maurice Hodgson† *Chairman ICI*	503·80	926·60	+83·9
Sir Terence Beckett† *Chairman Ford*	402·90	689·30	+71·0
Sir Leslie Murphy *Chairman NEB*	295·70	437·00	+47·8
Lord Denning *Master of the Rolls*	252·00	334·10	+32·6

*After deducting tax and national insurance on non-contracted out basis.
**Also before changes agreed in April.
†Figures based on last year's salary.

Effective tax

Secondly, there is the important difference between *effective* and *notional* tax liability. General tax allowances (such as child allowances) are worth more to higher income earners because they save them higher rates of taxation. On top of that, it is the same people who can make the most of additional tax relief, such as mortgages and life assurance. It is therefore patently absurd that the Royal Commission (Higher Incomes, para. 279) in their work assumes "no other reliefs and allowances" for the £10,000+ per year category, other than the mandatory child and personal allowances.

Labour Research Department August 1979

The overall impression is that income tax has made very little difference to the distribution of income. What difference there is as a result of the progressiveness of the tax system is soon cancelled out anyway by the impact of indirect taxes (taxes on goods, such as VAT, etc.) across the range of expenditure by different levels of income-earners. (Royal Commission, Standing Reference, para. 171)

It is commonly believed that the income tax structure is progressive, i.e. that greater proportions of higher incomes are claimed by taxation than of lower incomes, but this principle can be blunted over a period of time and also neutralised by other kinds of taxes.

Fringe benefits

Finally, mention must be made of fringe benefits. It is clear from the Royal Commission (Higher Incomes Report) that the value of fringe benefits, not only the company car and superannuation provisions, but also lunches and medical insurance, is very significant. And it is equally clear that the application of fringe benefits increases along with salary levels: the higher the position of the senior employee, the greater the proportion of his total financial well-being is derived from fringe benefits.

The effect of this pattern is to cancel out the redistributive impact of the taxation structure between high and low-paid and to restore to the former in post-tax terms the kind of differential they originally enjoyed in gross pay terms.

Topic 5 Taxation – Avoidance and evasion

New Statesman April 1979

Read and discuss

(1) What are the differences between direct and indirect taxation?
(2) As a proportion of their weekly income, which group pays more tax: higher or lower income groups?
(3) Are there 'no other reliefs' for the £10 000 plus income group?
(4) Has there been an increase in 'fringe benefits'?
(5) What is the difference between *notional* and *effective* taxation?
(6) What are the implications?
(7) Does the tax system benefit higher income earners? Compare tables A and B.
(8) Figure out how much of a wage increase (both gross and net) you would need to keep level with inflation.

Taxation
Political hypocrisy

Pressure for a comprehensive examination of the tax system is gaining momentum. The urgent need for reform was amply illustrated by Professor James Meade (chairman of the influential but independent committee on tax reform).

The current system is, he argues, riddled with "political hypocrisy." Egalitarians could satisfy themselves that the principles of equity and fairness were fulfilled by the existence of nominal marginal tax rates rising to 83p and 98p in the £. Those concerned most with economic efficiency and incentives could at the same time rest assured that hardly anyone actually has to pay such rates. Adequate governmental escape routes are provided in the form of legitimate loopholes, while those who have exhausted all such avenues have every incentive to engage in plain old-fashioned tax evasion. Those subject to the highest marginal "tax" rates from which there is no escape are over 50,000 families caught in the "poverty trap."

Economic efficiency also suffers under the current tax system. Savings and investments have been sucked into those areas singled out for favourable tax treatment—principally owner-occupied housing, life insurance and pension funds—rather than into more directly productive sectors. Earned income is taxed more heavily than unearned (since only the former is subject to national insurance contributions) and the only forms of wealth subjected to tax are those which yield income; "unproductive" assets (cars, yachts, houses) remain tax free.

Meanwhile, in the corporate sector, the proportion of total direct tax revenue contributed by companies was halved between 1966-1976; and mainstream corporation tax has now been virtually abolished for most commercial and industrial companies. Of the top 20 such companies, twelve paid no such tax at all last year (including BP, Esso, Rio-Tinto Zinc, Courtaulds, Grand Metropolitan, Dunlop, British Leyland and Ford). Mainstream corporation tax for these 20 companies averaged only 3½ per cent of their estimated £4,323 million profit in 1976.

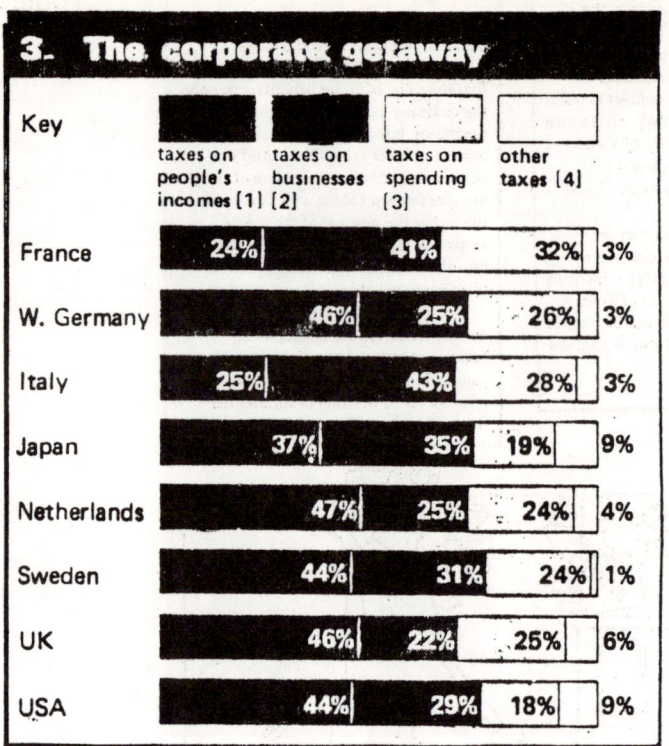

UK companies pay lower tax

In the UK the percentage of total taxation raised though corporation tax fell between 1970 and 1976, while in other countries (apart from Japan and Australia) there was little change. This has left UK companies paying a smaller proportion of total taxation (4.7 per cent) than companies in nearly all other western countries.

New Society 30 November 1978

Read and discuss

(1) How does overall tax in Britain compare with other countries?
(2) Do countries where tax is a higher percentage of gross domestic product do better or worse than Britain in terms of industrial performance?
(3) Of total Government revenue from taxation: How much comes from personal income/from business? (Compare with 10 years ago.)
(4) Why has corporation tax been halved in the past 10 years? (cf. 'Political hypocrisy')
(5) Why do British companies pay lower tax?

the tax myth
Reality: a charter for avoidance

The surreal character of Tory propaganda on the issue is conveyed by a report (*Observer*) that the Shadow Chancellor is expected to say during the campaign that he will reduce income tax 'to Common Market levels.' A glance at Table 1 (below) shows that on any proper reading, that would commit Sir Geoffrey Howe to increasing British taxation. To be sure, Sir Geoffrey probably intends nothing more, in reality, than a cut in the 83 per cent top rate on earned income – to which few are liable in theory, and scarcely anyone pays in practice. (Table 1): it is also clear that among those countries which out-tax us are several of those whose economies regularly out-perform our own. the figures for estate-duty and capital-transfer tax (CTT) show a decline from £1,055 million ten years ago to some £370 million today.

Total tax revenue for 1978-9 is estimated at £42 billion, of which £24 billion comes from the Inland Revenue: nearly all is income tax, with £4 billion corporation tax and a few scraps of surtax, capital gains tax and CTT. A STOCK ITEM of political debate is the idea that British industry staggers under a vast tax burden. If the personal tax system is rather a shambles, the corporate tax system is chaos enclosed in mythology, with most industrial companies paying little, if any, tax. John Kay and I found that of 20 leading UK industrial concerns, 13 paid *no* mainstream corporation tax in 1977, and in total only £117 million of tax was paid compared with total reported profits in 1976 of £4,276 million.³ The 'temporary' stock relief of November 1974 has survived almost five years, with no sign of a permanent solution. Because nothing has been announced, companies are uncertain about their tax liability, and so we have a tax which raises scarcely any revenue but yet generates economic distortions.

³ *The British Tax System*, J. A. Kay & M. A. King, Oxford

Labour Research Department

Read and discuss

(1) Do you think tax avoidance is underpublicised? If so, why?
(2) What is the difference between tax avoidance and tax evasion? (cf. Level 1 material on 'Social Myth'.)
(3) What are the implications of tax avoidance/evasion? Are either (a) morally (b) politically acceptable?
(4) Should those who earn more pay more tax?
(5) Does tax avoidance/evasion affect you (a) economically, (b) politically?

Written work (for whole of Taxation topic)

(1) How are any inequalities of wealth/income maintained? Give examples.
(2) Could the tax system be fairer? In what ways?

Longer written work

(1) 'The selfish pursuit of luxury is aided by the tax system'. Discuss.
(2) 'The tax system is a reflection of other inequalities'. Discuss.

Tax avoidance total may be £11 billions

By Victor Keegan, Business Editor

BRITAIN's "black economy" — the growing area of tax avoidance and "moonlighting" — may amount to as much as 7.5 per cent of the entire economy according to evidence given to the Commons Public Accounts Committee yesterday.

The figure, higher than most private estimates, was given in evidence by Sir William Pile, chairman of the Board of the Inland Revenue.

He emphasised it was not the product of an authoritative survey, which was impossible to do, but the result of consultation with senior colleagues.

They found it not implausible that undetected incomes could amount to 7.5 per cent of the gross domestic product whereas 15 per cent would be implausible.

If Sir William's "guestimate" is accurate it could mean that something like £11 billions of income each year is escaping income tax. If that could be collected it would increase tax receipts enough to clip over £2 billions (about 25 per cent) from the Public Sector Borrowing Requirement.

The importance of yesterday's figure is that it is the first time that a well-informed guess about the size of the black economy (which includes everything from an unincorporated company to a moonlighting plumber) has come from an authoritative government source.

Sir William said that he was sure that the black economy was large and that a deterioration had taken place over the past 10 years.

By contrast, Sir William pointed out that PAYE was the surest way of collecting tax because about 25 per cent is deducted every week from wages.

One of the problems about tax collecting, Sir William said, was that there were now two million unincorporated companies of which the Revenue could cursorily examine nine per cent and, in detail, only three per cent.

In about 8 per cent of the last cases, there was clearly something wrong but where the amount was less than £300 the Revenue was inclined not to pursue the matter.

Guardian November 1978

Bradman hit £18·2m off Wimpey tax

GEORGE WIMPEY & Co., the big international contractor, may have wiped out the better part of its 1976 tax bill—possibly as much as £18.2m—by using a complex tax avoidance scheme marketed by Godfrey Bradman's London Mercantile Corporation.

Documents filed at Companies House show that Rossminster Group Holdings, whose own complicated avoidance schemes were detailed by Business News a year ago, was also involved in some of the dizzying Wimpey deals.

The cost to Wimpey was £2.8m —a fee which was to be paid to a company in turn controlled by an unusual charitable trust.

Sunday Times 29 May 1977

£500M lent to tax avoiders

By STUART MANSELL

Loans totalling £500 millions have been made by a fringe merchant bank to support the tax avoidance schemes of Mr Roy Tucker, the Mayfair tax accountant. The schemes, disclosed in the Guardian earlier this week, involve circular flow of money between the unquoted investment bankers Rossminster Group, and Mr Tucker's companies, Brindonian and Richstock.

The purpose is to reduce corporation tax liabilities of client companies by using a loophole in the tax regulations.

Sunday Times 29 May 1977

Design

Design the front page of a mass circulation daily dealing with tax evaders as those 'who hold the country to ransom'.

Research (for a possible *project*)

What is the relationship between profits and investments? From the library, locate the annual accounts of five large firms in Britain.
Compare the profits with the rate of investment over the past 5 or 10 years.

Level 3

Subject Area: Ideology

The use of ideology to sustain power structures and maintain social control.
(This will reflect on some of the areas covered previously, mainly Social myth: What is falsely obvious; Mass communications and Political literacy.)

Aims

(1) To develop a critical awareness of the use of ideology.
(2) To demonstrate a conceptual ability.
(3) To identify the underlying principles in an argument.
(4) To collate, process and research information.
(5) To recognise and analyse appropriate sources of reference.
(6) To propose reasoned solutions to problems and assess alternative solutions.

Topic 1 Standpoints of History

Read and discuss

(1) What sort of history has the worker been reading? Has it been written from the standpoint of famous *individuals*?
(2) Marx defined history as 'the actions of men in pursuit of their ends....' Who writes history? Who makes it?
(3) Can you name any historians? From what standpoint has their work been written?
(4) Is the Brecht poem critical of the way in which some history has been recorded?
(5) Is much of today's history (contemporary politics, for example) as reflected in the mass media, written from the standpoint of famous individuals?
(6) Do famous individuals 'make' history or do they represent *groups* of people?

A WORKER READS HISTORY

Who built the seven gates of Thebes?
The books are filled with names of kings.
Was it kings who hauled the craggy blocks of stone?
And Babylon, so many times destroyed,
Who built the city up each time? In which of Lima's houses,
That city glittering with gold, lived those who built it?
In the evening when the Chinese wall was finished
Where did the masons go? Imperial Rome
Is full of arcs of triumph. Who reared them up? Over whom
Did the Caesars triumph? Byzantium lives in song,
Were all her dwellings palaces? And even in Atlantis of the legend
The night the sea rushed in,
The drowning men still bellowed for their slaves.

Young Alexander conquered India.
He alone?
Caesar beat the Gauls.
Was there not even a cook in his army?
Philip of Spain wept as his fleet
Was sunk and destroyed. Were there no other tears?
Frederick the Great triumphed in the Seven Years War. Who
Triumphed with him?

Each page a victory,
At whose expense the victory ball?
Every ten years a great man,
Who paid the piper?

So many particulars.
So many questions.

Bertolt Brecht

Topic 2 Caught in a catch-phrase

Here are two contrasting statements:

(1) Those who for political reasons dishonourably disrupt their contracts of service by indulging in industrial inaction (for some reason called industrial action) are surely admitting that they can stand the financial loss involved – which makes nonsense of some of their subsequently exaggerated wage claims. Further, they are seriously damaging the reputation of this country abroad.

(2) Men in the lowest position are usually uninformed as to the nature of the work they have to do, especially in construction work. From force of habit they have learned that they will be told at the last moment when to go to work, and at the last moment when they are no longer needed – in other words, you need not return tomorrow. It is also true that they are kept standing about a great deal of the time....
Instead of endlessly disposing of people as materials, it might do well to show them, for instance, where their work fits in with the total work-structure. It would relieve them of the pressure of false presence, of having to appear to do when there is actually nothing to do. False presence is the most prevalent of modern diseases; it is a planned murder beside which war is of little consequence.

Written work

(1) What type of person would have made each statement. (Occupation is an important consideration.)
(2) What are the differences in attitudes being expressed?
(3) What values are implied in each? Which would attract you? Why?

Discussion (after discussion of written work)

Align the following common statements into separate *systems of beliefs*. Discuss also where the two statements above would fit:

Everybody starts as equals: the self-made man is the backbone

> ideology A system of ideas defined by its function in a social structure, and not by its status as knowledge. To say that some ideas form an ideology is to claim that their acceptance supports the existence or furthers the interests of a social group; it is not to allege that the ideas are true or false, sincerely or insincerely held, statements of fact or value-judgements. (But ideological analysis may involve discussing truth, sincerity, etc.; whether, and how ideas support a social group can depend in part on such issues.)

from *Language and Social Reality*,
Open University Press, p.76

of society: the union is the only protection for working people: there are equal opportunities for everybody — it's your own fault if you don't take them: trade unions hold the country to ransom: the State should leave private enterprise to get on with it: the 'national interest' is always a management interest: the class system ensures and maintains inequality: only collective ownership of the means of production can solve social problems: the country is run by public school twits.

These conflicting systems of belief constitute opposing *ideologies*.

Further written work

(1) Write an article for the front page of a mass circulation daily identifying the 'national interest' with public sector workers' case for a minimum wage.

Answers to questions on p.101:

(1) Statement by Sir Halford Reddish, Chairman of Rugby Portland Cement at the Annual General Meeting in 1973. Quoted from the *Birmingham Post* 25 April, 1973.
(2) From '*By the Sound*', a novel by Edward Dorn about construction workers in Washington State (previously called 'Rites of Passage') pp. 175–7, *Frontier Press*, Massachusetts, USA, 1971.

(i) Examples of use of ideology
(1) Power workers' demands threaten the social contract.
(2) GEC's future threatened by strikes.
(3) Traffic disrupted again by demonstrations.

Here are the same ideas, written from a different standpoint:
(1) MP's pay settlement endangers social contract.
(2) GEC's future threatened by huge dividend payouts.
(3) Traffic disrupted by Queen's procession.

Assume both sets of statements are true
(1) Which are more common? Why?
(2) Do some of the statements have such mass currency that their opposites appear to be (a) freakish, (b) untrue?
(3) What is the *social function* of the first set of statements?

History/Herstory

(ii) Another example
How much of your attitudes are determined by the way in which you receive news?

IDEOLOGY

'There are no women artists'

When people first look at the miniature illustrated here, they assume it portrays a courtly lady putting on makeup. (Fig. I, 1) Closer scrutiny shows her brush to be pointing the other way, outward, and indeed it is a fanciful reconstruction of Marcia, a Roman artist, in the process of doing her self-portrait.

Fig. I, 1 Marcia, depicted painting a self-portrait. 1402.

Women Artists
The Women's Press, London 1976

Marcia *is* a painter (note the date)
If you were given a different view of history
(of which women artists are merely a part)
would your views and attitudes be different?

Topic 3 Making your Mark

REPORT of the Commissioners of Police of the Metropolis for the Year 1977. HMSO, Cmnd 7238 (June 1978). £2.10.

Public order is central to the Report. But is it really the dominant operational burden that is claimed? During 1977, 51,692 working days were lost to the Metropolitan Police through injury on duty. Of these, 3,482 were due to 'injuries received while controlling crowds'.

If you saw a newspaper headline: *3 482 Police Injuries while controlling crowds!* What would you think?
(1) That more police power was needed to control demonstrations?
(2) That demonstrations should be banned?
(3) That the police are the unfortunate group 'in the middle' maintaining law and order?
(4) That courts should be more severe?

In other words, would the use by the paper, of information from the annual report, be attempting to advance certain arguments?
If so, this would be an example of ideological usage. (See the definition of ideology.)

Now read the rest of that part of the annual report.

This category includes not only events like anti-NF demonstrations and Grunwicks but also the control of football crowds. Furthermore, the 3,482 figure compares with 6,235 days lost due to motor-cycle accidents when the injured officer was riding on duty and 6,342 days lost due to accidents when the injured officer was on duty in a car.
In addition, a further 6,057 days were lost through officers' off-duty injuries in sports and games. The point here is that public order is *singled out as* creating intolerable burdens on police manpower. The facts do not justify this singling-out. The purpose of highlighting public order is quite simply to make a political point.

State Research Bulletin

Written work

Find other examples, in any mass communication, of the use of partial information as ideology.

Topic 4 Making up your mind...(for you)

> 'THE PROBLEMS OF British Leyland', have come to be defined on the television news as the difficulty of preventing workers taking part in 'avoidable stoppages'. This was first demonstrated in a study carried out in 1975*. Quite what effect the continuing focus has had on viewers is hard to ascertain. But when one sees banners at a Wembley Cup Final proclaiming 'Mike Channon strikes quicker than British Leyland', it suggests that something is happening at the level of popular consciousness.
>
> The same study showed that nearly 40 per cent of reports on industry were related to strikes. So it was no surprise to find that when British Leyland cropped up in the news again in February 1979, the topic was again a strike.
>
> *Research by the Glasgow University Media Group, published in Bad News, Routledge and Kegan Paul.

> On 7 February, workers at the Longbridge plant in Birmingham came out on unofficial strike. They said they were protesting at the management's refusal to make back-dated payments which had been agreed by both sides in return for higher levels of productivity. In the context of the agreement the unions had conceded that redundancies could take place. The shop stewards pointed out that 7,000 redundancies had occurred and claimed that the management was attempting to conceal the true levels of production at both Austin-Morris and Jaguar. Management claimed that productivity had not been high enough to justify the payments, that the men had misunderstood the terms of the agreement and that the shop stewards were breaking the procedure agreement. Given that both sides had competing explanations to offer, in principle each of these might have been explored. In the main, however, coherence and rationality were granted to management views and not to those of the workforce.

Read and discuss

(1) Consider industrial disputes you have seen reported on television. Have they been reported like this one?
(2) How 'balanced' have they been? 'Balance should mean equal coverage *of the same nature* of both sides.

> Industrial correspondents do their own scene-setting in between headlines, interviews and selected quotes from ministers. Iain Ross, for example, relays the management view of the strike on 7 February:
>
>> BL management wasn't slow to blast back at the Longbridge stewards for acting unconstitutionally, breaking procedure, overturning the secret ballot vote and spreading inaccurate information.
>
> Ross then refers to productivity figures without mentioning the union's claims that productivity was higher at Austin Morris and at Jaguar (these were discussed on the *Tonight* programme, 12 February, but not on the main news):
>
>> Now the extra productivity is measured against output in 1977 – goodness knows, a bad year for disputes...
>>
>> An all-out strike could mean BL revising the corporate plan it's submitted to the NEB, cutting back investment, cutting back jobs. The failure of British car companies to produce cars means a boost for imports which we learn accounted for 54 per cent of all sales last month, when, incidentally, BL cars were market leader for the fourth consecutive month.
>
> BL management, having avoided the kind of challenge thrown at Robinson, emerges as the victim – having to revise the corporate plan and cut jobs and investment because of the strike. There is no room for an alternative view. That last phrase – 'BL were market leaders for the fourth consecutive month' – is treated, quite literally, as incidental information. In an alternative frame it could have been used to contradict, or at least to challenge, the conventional view that BL is failing to produce cars because of frequent strikes.

New Statesman
May 1979

Open Questions?

Interviewing approaches to the two groups were strikingly different. Interviews with Pat Lowry, personnel director of BL Cars, and Ray Horrocks, managing director of Austin-Morris, began with open invitations to them to elaborate on their views. When they did so, their views were allowed to stand without interruption or challenge. On the rare occasions when a second question was put to them it was encouraging rather than challenging. Thus, on 7 February, BBC1's Iain Ross interviewed Horrocks:

Ross: When I spoke to the boss of Austin-Morris, of which Longbridge is the biggest part, I asked him if the workers had been deliberately misled by the stewards.

Horrocks: I am saying that they were given the wrong information without *any* shadow of doubt at all and that is now very evident. Because against the background of the *same* information, 66,000 in 27 plants right across the country have voted to stay at work.

Ross: So what's the message *in that* for Longbridge?

On ITN, Geoffrey Green introduced Horrocks with these words:

Green: If Longbridge doesn't go back, Leyland say other plants are going to be hit. And there is a long-term threat too.

Horrocks: In what I think is the unlikely event that Longbridge stay out – there's no doubt at all in my mind, I shall have to ask the Chief Executive of BL Limited that I should re-appraise the Austin-Morris plant and that will have long term implications for the company.

Green: What sort of implications? ...

Closed Questions?

The aggressive questions put to shop stewards and pickets stand out in marked contrast. A typical example was when Peter Colbourne of BBC1 interviewed Derek Robinson, convenor of shop stewards at Longbridge, on 7 February. Robinson attempted to reject the interpretive framework of the interviewer, who failed to acknowledge the points he was making and persisted in the assumptions with which he had begun:

Colbourne: The vote was in favour of an instant walk-out. There have been dire warnings that another stoppage could spell the end of British Leyland. After this one would there be a plant or a job to come back to?

Robinson: I'm confident we shall have a plant and a job to go back to. I note that Mr Edwardes might not have a job. Indeed, he's already seeking tax exile. I wish that some of our members on the wages that we get could seek tax exile, at the same rate as himself.

Colbourne: Leyland workers over recent years have got a reputation with the public for perhaps doing things very quickly and doing sometimes stupid things – is this one of them?

Robinson: I wouldn't have thought so. But you know, you were here last year when we persuaded our members not to. If anyone's adopted a responsible attitude it's the workers at Longbridge.

Colbourne: Was it responsible to go ahead with *this* strike?

In a similar vein, David Smith interviewed Robinson on ITN on 8 February.

Smith: There were clashes this morning between pickets and drivers trying to get building materials through to a plant that will build the new Mini – the car that is the key to the company's future. Aren't the men cutting their own throats?

Robinson: We're on strike. It's been forced upon us. We've got no alternative. And we intend to use the full force of our membership in picketing this plant to ensure that nothing moves in and nothing moves out. We *regret* that we have to do these things. But until such time as the management come down to earth, that's how it will continue.

Smith: Even if it destroys the company? ...

Written work

(1) What is the function of this type of reporting?
(2) Write an interview (a) using open questions, (b) closed questions. You will need to be clear about what exactly you are trying to prove before framing the questions.

How different would public attitudes to trade unions be if media coverage of them was different?
Does the cartoon portray media coverage of unions as manipulative: that is, using power in exactly the same way as unions are accused of; to convey certain attitudes?

"...the unions are so powerful soon they will be telling us what to think..."

Topic 5 The old school tie (1)

Hooray! The chaps are back

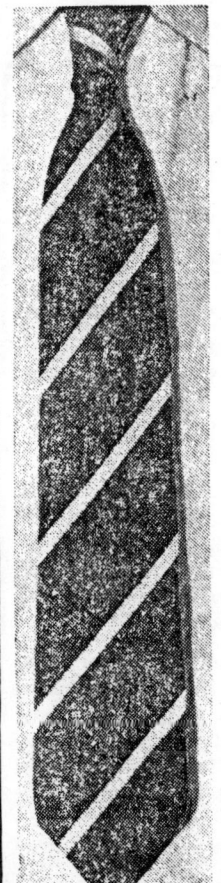

RECOGNISE THIS tie? Let's be perfectly frank about it. Probably not.

However, there's one thing you can be sure about. An awful lot of the chaps in Mrs. Thatcher's new Government, should their eyes stray to this page, will recognise it as quick as you can say *Floreat Etona*.

Is the suspense killing you? We will put you out of your misery forthwith. *Floreat Etona* is the Eton motto. And, of course, that's the Old Etonian tie.

Yes, the ruling classes are well and truly back in power.

Quiet in class, please, for the roll call. Pray step forward:

The Right Honourables Francis Pym, Sir Ian Gilmour and David Howell, plus Messrs Douglas Hurd, Nicholas Ridley, Adam Butler, Jerry Wiggin, Michael Allison, Paul Channon, Spencer le Marchant, Anthony Berry, Peter Morrison, baronet Sir George Young and duke's son Lord James Douglas-Hamilton, whose title does not debar him from the Commons.

Plus My Lords Hailsham, Carrington, Soames, Trenchard, Strathcona, Belstead, Gowrie, Mansfield, Elton and Denham.

Old Etonians, every one. All in the Government. All twenty-four.

Are we preaching old-fashioned class warfare?

Not at all. We're just stating the remarkable fact.

We wish them well. Our goodwill hasn't run out only ten days after their notable victory. Perhaps now that they're back where they belong (or so they honestly believe), they'll cheer up a bit about dear old Britain.

In their view, the very fact that they are in command again has already helped to restore Britain's greatness.

Who knows, before long some of them may be singing the praises of British Leyland, whose factory for the new Mini is the world's most modern. Even the Japanese have been to look at it, as the Daily Express reported on Polling Day (a bit late).

Joy upon joys, Britain may even win the America's Cup with the fabulous new yacht Lionheart, made by British craftsmen *(who else?)*

Good times must surely be ahead, even if one notable ex-grammar school boy is left out in the cold.

So there you are, Mum and Dad. If you want your son to get ahead in politics, you know where to send him.

And if you have a little girl? Well, try a grammar school like Kesteven and Grantham.

Its former head girl is in charge of the aforementioned lot.

PS *Floreat Etona* means "May Eton Flourish." You can say that again.

Sunday Mirror May 1979

Read and discuss

(1) Establish the tone of the editorial.
(2) Is the 'remarkable fact' a *fact*? Can it be verified?
(3) Does it matter what school the people went to?
(4) Does the article inform or manipulate or both?
(5) How adequately does it inform its readers?
(6) What is its function?

The old school tie (2)

Read and discuss

(1) Does this information shed a different light on the '*Mirror*' editorial?
(2) What are the connections between education and occupation?
(3) Does a certain type of background appear to lead to certain positions of power?
(4) Bring up to date the figures for the schools mentioned.

Longer written work

Trace the connections between the distribution of wealth and equality of opportunity in contemporary Britain.
This will involve further research. The library should have the necessary books.

Education

A child who goes to a fee-paying school gets the benefit of much smaller classes and therefore much more individual attention than in a state school. Fee-paying schools fall into two categories: (1) Independent schools where the full fees are paid; these include the public schools, like Eton, where, in 1972, the annual fee was £861, Harrow (£867), Winchester (£972) and Gordonstoun (£948). (2) Direct grant schools which are subsidised direct by the government and which are part fee-paying and part free places provided by the local authority. These two categories of fee-paying schools take 4 per cent of all children. The other 96 per cent go to local authority maintained schools.

The result of the inequality in staffing is that children at fee-paying schools have a far better chance of reaching university than those at ordinary schools. The following table shows the destination of school leavers in 1970-71. It shows, for example, that a child at an independent fee-paying school has 19 times as great a chance of getting to Oxford or Cambridge as a child at a local authority school.

DESTINATION ON LEAVING SCHOOL (1970–71)

	Local authority maintained schools	Direct grant schools	Independent recognised fee-paying
Number of leavers (thousands)	572·03	15·40	25·99
Percentage going to:			
Oxford or Cambridge	0·3	6·4	5·7
Other universities	4·4	27·9	16·2
Total universities	4·7	34·3	21·9
Other full-time further education	14·2	30·6	37·9
Employment	81·1	35·1	40·2

Source: *Education Statistics 1971*, Vol 2.

A public-school education followed by an Oxford or Cambridge degree is still the best passport to the highest paid and most influential jobs.

Less than 4 per cent of all children get such an education. Yet of 81 judges in 1972 (House of Lords, Court of Appeal, Chancery Division and Queen's Bench) no less than 62 (76 per cent) went to public schools. One went to a direct grant school, 13 to grammar or other council schools (16 per cent); about 5 there is no information. No less than 66 of the 81 went either to Oxford or Cambridge.

Of the 23 top jobs in the Foreign and Commonwealth Office (permanent under-secretaries, deputy under-secretaries, assistant under-secretaries) at least 15 (or 65 per cent) were educated at public schools and 19 out of the 23 went to Oxford or Cambridge.

Of the 22 generals and lieutenant-generals in 1972, 18 went to public schools. Out of the 17 admirals and vice-admirals, 15 went to public schools. Only the top jobs in the air force appear to go less frequently to ex-public schoolboys. Of 20 air chief marshals and air marshals 8 went to public schools (40 per cent) 8 to grammar or council schools, one to a direct grant school, one was educated abroad, and two do not say where they were educated.

The latest comprehensive investigation into the social background of the administrative civil service was done for the Fulton Committee on the Civil Service and published in 1969. The result was summed up by Lord Fulton, chairman of the committee, who said that the survey had shown that "79 per cent of direct recruits into the top echelons of the service were of upper and middle class backgrounds . . . 56 per cent of the top administrators were educated at fee-paying schools, and two thirds came from Oxford and Cambridge" (*Times* 7.5.69).

News of the World, March 5, 1978

COMMENT

The Great Divider

SUDDENLY, the once-Sunny Jim Callaghan is behaving like a loser.

He wades into the Tory leadership with the charge that they are out to split Britain. He accuses:

❝They divide society so that those who draw social security are called scroungers; redundancy payments are for shirkers; trade unionists are dictators; and the blacks are swamping us.❞

Only a politician who has lost his common touch can let fly with such a savaging of the decent multitude who believe the evidence of their eyes and ears. Namely that:

● Too much social security money DOES go to scroungers.

● Too much redundancy money DOES go to people who walk straight into other jobs.

● Too many trade union bosses ARE dictators.

● There HAS been more immigration than Britain can comfortably absorb.

Can there be any doubt that it is Mr Callaghan himself who is The Great Divider?

Topic 6   Freedom of the editorial

Are the four main points mentioned here facts or assertions?
Could they be proved?
What is their *function*: do they act as 'news', comment or what?
Does the presentation of information this way inform or manipulate?
How adequately does this editorial inform its readers?
Does it provide 'balance'?

The lack 'of common touch' seems to be the ultimate proof of the editorial.
Can it be defined?
How useful is it as a tool of political analysis?
Does it always denote a conservative attitude?
Have you ever used the phrase 'common sense...' in an argument?
In what circumstances?
What type of appeal is being made?

The central accusation is that Mr Callaghan is a 'great divider'.
What do you think is the intention of the editorial?
Would it have a divisive effect?
What *system of beliefs* do the four editorial points fit into?

Written work

(1) Can the following information prove/disprove the editorial point about redundancy?
(2) From your library get a copy of the *Department of Employment* gazette. Find out the number of redundancies in your area: write an essay on the social effects.

Longer written work

Interview four people in your area who have been made redundant. Pay particular attention to whether they (a) agree/disagree with the point in the editorial, and (b) if they see any connection between redundancy money and obtaining (where possible) new jobs.

What price a lost job?

REDUNDANCY PAY

The basic entitlement *EPCA Sch 4*

To pay a redundant worker his/her due compensation the employer has to make the following allowance by reckoning back from the date due statutory notice runs out:

- $1\frac{1}{2}$ *weeks' pay* for each complete year of employment between the ages of 41 and 65 (60 for women);
- *1 week's pay* for each complete year of employment between 22 and 40;
- $\frac{1}{2}$ *week's pay* for each complete year of employment between 18 and 21

As an example, take the case of a 50 year old man with 15 years' continuous employment. He has served nine years in the 41-65 bracket ($1\frac{1}{2}$ weeks' pay for each year) and six years in the 22-40 bracket (1 week's pay for each year). So the calculation is:

$9 \times 1\frac{1}{2}$ weeks' pay
plus $\quad = \quad 19\frac{1}{2}$ weeks' pay
6×1 week's pay

Who pays for redundancy compensation?

Employers do not pay for all of the statutory redundancy payments they make. At present any employer who makes a payment required by the RPA can claim back 41 per cent from a central fund — the **Redundancy Fund.** Set up in 1965 by the RPA the Redundancy Fund is financed by the state and by employers out of the earnings-related contributions. An employer who makes a redundancy payment to someone who would not otherwise qualify for one (eg someone who failed to claim in time) can *still* get a rebate from the Fund. Employers who pay into the Fund in respect of workers in the "excluded" category are entitled to a rebate when they make their own non-statutory redundancy payments.

£100,000 for this man

The average is £620

In 1977, some 267,233 redundancies were noted by the Department of Employment, and that figure has now been swelled by closures at Spillers, British Leyland and Thorn's consumer electronics division. Last year, the nation's redundancy fund, financed from social security contributions, paid out £88m, and at this rate 1978's bill will be even higher.

Payments to individuals vary widely. Commercial Union's chief executive, Gordon Dunlop, (pictured above right) who resigned after policy differences last year, has just been given £100,000 as an "ex gratia payment for loss of office."

By comparison, British Leyland has been offering men at its doomed Speke plant an average of only £1,500, with certain payments as low as £400, although the unions are trying to improve these terms.

Sunday Times 30 April 1978

Joe left Poland in 1939. Since coming to Britain after the war he has had a score of jobs, from coalminer to labourer on the M5, before joining British Steel 10 years ago. At East Moors he was first a crane greaser, then a bricklayer's helper. In a good year, when British Steel was pouring out steel and there was overtime, he earned £5,000 a year. In his last year he earned £80 to £90 a week. He got a £6,000 redundancy payment.

Joe, now 58, is divorced and pays £2.50 maintenance to his wife (his daughter is married). He spent his £6,000 on buying his house. He has not looked for a job yet because he wanted to do up the house and there was no financial need. Next spring he knows he must try to find something. By then he will be living off his £10-a-week pension.

"I'd much rather be back at the works than have the house. I was saving up to buy one anyway and think that within four or five years I would have saved enough. Look at it this way, that £6,000 was only just over a year's wages. If the job had gone on I could have earned £5,000 a year for the next eight years until retiring age and that would have been £40,000."

The Queen and the Duke of Edinburgh are framed on one side of the mantlepiece;

Guardian 3 October 1979

Topic 7 Equality – More equal than whom?

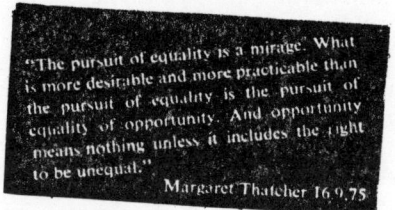

"The pursuit of equality is a mirage. What is more desirable and more practicable than the pursuit of equality is the pursuit of equality of opportunity. And opportunity means nothing unless it includes the right to be unequal."
Margaret Thatcher 16.9.75

Envy is capable of serving the valuable social function of making the rich moderate their habits for fear of arousing it. It is because of the existence of envy that one does not drive Rolls-Royces through the slums of Naples.

Equality. Sir Keith Joseph and Jonathan Sumption. John Murray £4.95

'To criticize inequality and to desire equality is not, as is sometimes suggested, to cherish the romantic illusion that men are equal in character and intelligence. It is to hold that, while their natural endowments differ profoundly, it is the mark of a civilised society to aim at eliminating such inequalities as have their source not in individual differences, but in its own organisation, and that individual differences which are a source of social energy, are more likely to ripen and find expression if social inequalities are, as far as practicable, diminished'.
Equality by R. H. Tawney

None of these statements is true or false.
They are value judgements. It would be better to judge them on their usefulness or limitation.
But they are, more than likely, part of conflicting *systems of belief*.

Read and discuss

(1) Is the pursuit of equality a 'mirage'?
(2) Is the first statement a closed circle? Can there be equality of opportunity *and* the right to be unequal?
(3) Identify political parties which would use the slogan 'the right to be unequal'. (See 'Political Literacy')
(4) Why is envy ascribed only to the non-rich? (statement 2)
(5) How conspicuous is wealth in this country? (See 'Distribution of Wealth')
(6) Is statement 2 an adequate defence of wealth?
(7) Statement 3: Are inequalities a product of 'social organisation'?
(8) Is it the mark of a 'civilised society to aim at eliminating inequalities'?

Discussion work leading to written work

(1) What other beliefs do you think would accompany statements 1 and 2: statement 3?
(2) What type of ideology would either system of beliefs represent?

Written work

(1) Write short essays (a) justifying inequality, (b) in support of equality. In each case discuss what changes may have to be made in the social structure.

Longer written work

Write a long essay on the problems of tackling any inequalities of opportunity you perceive as necessary.

Overall longer written work (Essay titles)

(1) 'There are no such things as facts, only ideological properties'. Discuss.
(2) 'Ignorance is the greatest form of social control'. Discuss.
(3) 'Being adequately informed means not being manipulated'. Discuss.
(4) 'Balance is not possible without equal power'. Discuss.